LABRADOODLE AND LABRADOODLES

The Ultimate Labradoodle Guide

Includes Mini Labradoodle, Australian Labradoodle, Labradoodle Puppies, Labradoodle Rescue, Labradoodle Breeders, and More!

By Susanne Saben
© DYM Worldwide Publishers

DYM Worldwide Publishers

ISBN: 978-1-911355-14-4

Published by DYM Worldwide Publishers 2016.

responsibility for errors, omissions, or contrary interpretation of the subject matter herein. Any perceived slights to any specific person(s) or organization(s) are purely unintentional. We have no control over the nature, content, and availability of the websites listed in this book. The inclusion of any website links does not necessarily imply a recommendation or endorse the views expressed within them. DYM Worldwide Publishers takes no responsibility for, and will not be liable for, the websites being temporarily or being removed from the Internet. The accuracy and completeness of the information provided herein and opinions stated herein are not guaranteed or warranted to produce any particular results, and the advice or strategies, contained herein may not be suitable for every individual. The author, publisher, distributors, and/or affiliates shall not be liable for any loss incurred as a consequence of the use and application, directly or indirectly of any information presented in this work. This publication is designed to provide information in regards to the subject matter covered. The information included in this book has been compiled to give an overview of the topics covered. The information contained in this book has been compiled to provide an overview of the subject. It is not intended as medical advice and should not be construed as such. For a firm diagnosis of any medical conditions you should consult a doctor or veterinarian (as related to animal health). The writer,

Foreword

What do you get when you cross a beautiful Poodle with a lively Labrador Retriever? The best dog breed imaginable, of course, The Labradoodle.

The Labradoodle is beautiful breed known for its curly coat and friendly personality. These dogs are the definition of "man's best friend" and I am personally lucky enough to own two of them! I have enjoyed the company of my Labradoodles so much that I just had to share my experience in the hopes of helping potential dog owners like you become more familiar with this amazing breed.

The Labradoodle is by far one of my favorite dog breeds and in reading this book, I hope that you will come to see why. I also hope that you might be inspired to bring home a Labradoodle puppy for yourself or your family! These dogs are absolutely gorgeous and full of life and personality, so they make excellent family pets. But don't just take my word for it – keep reading to learn everything you need to know about Labradoodles and to decide whether they just might be the perfect pet that you and your family have been looking for!

Table of Contents

Chapter One: Introduction to Labradoodles 1

Useful Terms to Know 4

Chapter Two: Labradoodle Temperament Breed and
Overview 9

1.) What is a Labradoodle Dog? 11

a.) Labrador Retriever Breed Overview 11

Summary of Labrador Retriever Facts 14

b.) Poodle Breed Overview 16

Summary of Poodle Breed Info 19

2.) Labradoodle Information and Facts 22

Summary of Labradoodle Facts 26

3.) Labradoodle Breed History 29

4.) Labradoodle Types and Sizes 30

a.) American Labradoodle 30

b.) Australian Labradoodle 31

c.) Standard Labradoodle 32

d.) Mini Labradoodle or Miniature Labradoodle 32

e.) Toy Labradoodle or Small Labradoodle 33

5.) Labradoodle Dog Colors and Pictures of Labradoodles
.... 34

a.) Chocolate Labradoodle 34

b.) Black Labradoodle 35

c.) Golden Labradoodle 35

d.) Red Labradoodle 36

e.) White Labradoodle 36

f.) Apricot Labradoodle 37

Chapter Three: Labrador Poodle Information 38

1.) Do You Need a License? 40

2.) Do Labradoodles Get Along with Other Pets? 42

3.) How Many Labradoodles Should You Get? 44

4.) Labradoodle Prices and Costs 45

a.) Initial Costs for Labradoodle Puppies 45

b.) Monthly Costs for Adult Labradoodles 51

5.) Labrador Poodle Pros and Cons 54

Chapter Four: Where to Find Labradoodle Breeders and
Labradoodle Puppies for Sale..56

1.) Where to Look for American Labradoodle Breeders..58

2.) Where to Find Australian Labradoodle Breeders and
Australian Labradoodle Puppies 62

3.) How to Pick a Healthy Labradoodle Puppy 65

a.) Precautions for Miniature Labradoodle Puppies for
Sale...67

4.) Pros and Cons of Labradoodle Adoption....................69

a.) Where to Find Labradoodle Rescues and Labradoodles for Adoption 71

Chapter Five: Labradoodle Dog Care Guide 74

1.) Labradoodle Home Requirements 75

a.) Setting Up a Space for Your Labradoodle................75

b.) Labradoodle Energy and Exercise Needs 77

c.) Recommended Labradoodle Accessories.................79

2.) Labradoodle Dog Nutrition...82

a.) Nutritional Needs for Labradoodle Dogs 85

b.) Choosing a Healthy Dog Food................................88

c.) Tips for Feeding Labradoodles 92

d.) Dangerous Foods to Avoid for Dogs.......................94

3.) Labradoodle Grooming Information 96

a.) Brushing and Bathing Your Labradoodle 97

b.) Cleaning Your Labradoodle's Ears 99

c.) Brushing Your Labradoodle's Teeth 99

d.) Clipping Your Dog's Nails......................................100

Chapter Six: Labradoodle Training Guide 102

1.) Overview of Popular Training Methods 104

2.) The Best Labradoodle Training Style........................108

3.) Labradoodle Crate Training Guide 112

Chapter Seven: Labradoodle Breeding and Labradoodle

Puppies 116

1.) General Labradoodle Breeding Information..............118

a.) What is an F1b Labradoodle? Hybrid Genetics.....118

b.) Basic Dog Breeding Information 119

c.) Breeding Risks and Precautions..........................121

2.) Raising Labradoodle Puppies 123

Chapter Eight: Labradoodle Health and Care Guide 128

1.) Common Health Problems for Labradoodles............130

2.) Labradoodle Vaccination Schedule 146

Chapter Nine: Showing Labradoodle Dogs 149

1.) Showing Mixed Breed Dogs...............................151

2.) Tips for Showing Your Labradoodle.....................153

Chapter Ten: Labradoodle Dog Care Sheet....................157

1.) Labradoodle Information Overview 159

2.) Labradoodle Home Requirements Overview...........161

3.) Labradoodle Nutritional Information....................163

4.) Labradoodle Breeding Information.......................165

Conclusion...167

Index..169

Chapter One: Introduction to Labradoodles

Cute and fluffy, the Labradoodle is known just as much for its beautiful wavy coat as for its friendly personality.

When it comes to choosing a dog breed, many people become overwhelmed by the sheer volume of options available to them. Do you go with a breed known for its friendly personality and gentle temperament or do you pick one that is known for its intelligence or for its beautiful coat and color? If you find yourself asking these very same questions, you may be glad to know that there is a single breed that contains all of these wonderful qualities. Which breed am I talking about? The Labradoodle!

The Labradoodle is a designer dog that comes from a crossing of a Labrador Retriever and a Poodle – does the name make sense now? I can tell you from personal experience that the Labradoodle possesses some of the best qualities of each parent breed and that this dog breed is entirely unique from all others. I should know because I have two of my own! I brought home my first Labradoodle puppy nearly six years ago now, and I immediately loved him so much that I had to get another!

Having been a proud Labradoodle owner for more than half a decade, it is fair to say that I know a lot about this breed. Designer dogs can be tricky sometimes since they are a cross between two pure breeds, but I happen to like surprises! From the moment I brought home each of my little bundles of love, I was enamored with the breed, and I wanted nothing more than to share my love with the world. That is where this book comes in! It is my goal and my sincere hope to help spread the word about the Labradoodle breed and to bring other dog owners like you into the fold. I am absolutely certain that once you learn about the many things, there are to love for the Labradoodle breed that you will become a believer yourself!

So, if you are ready to learn more about the Labradoodle breed and what makes it such a wonderful pet, then I encourage you to turn the page and keep reading. Let's get to it!

Useful Terms to Know

AKC – American Kennel Club, the largest purebred dog registry in the United States

Almond Eye – Referring to an elongated eye shape rather than a rounded shape

Apple Head – A round-shaped skull

Balance – A show term referring to all of the parts of the dog, both moving and standing, which produce a harmonious image

Beard – Long, thick hair on the dog's underjaw

Best in Show – An award given to the only undefeated dog left standing at the end of judging

Bitch – A female dog

Bite – The position of the upper and lower teeth when the dog's jaws are closed; positions include level, undershot, scissors, or overshot

Blaze – A white stripe running down the center of the face between the eyes

Board – To house, feed, and care for a dog for a fee

Breed – A domestic race of dogs having a common gene pool and characterized appearance/function

Breed Standard – A published document describing the look, movement, and behavior of the perfect specimen of a particular breed

Buff – An off-white to gold coloring

Clip – A method of trimming the coat in some breeds

Coat – The hair covering of a dog; some breeds have two coats, and outer coat and undercoat; also known as a double coat. Examples of breeds with double coats include German Shepherd, Siberian Husky, Akita, etc.

Condition – The health of the dog as shown by its skin, coat, behavior, and general appearance

Crate – A container used to house and transport dogs; also called a cage or kennel

Crossbreed (Hybrid) – A dog having a sire and dam of two different breeds; cannot be registered with the AKC

Dam (bitch) – The female parent of a dog

Designer Dog – A dog breed created by crossing two pure breeds.

Dock – To shorten the tail of a dog by surgically removing the end part of the tail.

Double Coat – Having an outer weather-resistant coat and a soft, waterproof coat for warmth; see above.

Drop Ear – An ear in which the tip of the ear folds over and hangs down; not prick or erect

Entropion – A genetic disorder resulting in the upper or lower eyelid turning in

Fancier – A person who is especially interested in a particular breed or dog sport

Fawn – A red-yellow hue of brown

Feathering – A long fringe of hair on the ears, tail, legs, or body of a dog

Groom – To brush, trim, comb or otherwise make a dog's coat neat in appearance

Heel – To command a dog to stay close by its owner's side

Hip Dysplasia – A condition characterized by the abnormal formation of the hip joint

Inbreeding – The breeding of two closely related dogs of one breed

Kennel – A building or enclosure where dogs are kept

Litter – A group of puppies born at one time

Markings – A contrasting color or pattern on a dog's coat

Mask – Dark shading on the dog's foreface

Mate – To breed a dog and a bitch

Neuter – To castrate a male dog or spay a female dog

Pads – The tough, shock-absorbent skin on the bottom of a dog's foot

Parti-Color – A coloration of a dog's coat consisting of two or more definite, well-broken colors; one of the colors must be white

Pedigree – The written record of a dog's genealogy going back three generations or more

Pied – A coloration on a dog consisting of patches of white and another color

Prick Ear – Ear that is carried erect, usually pointed at the tip of the ear

Puppy – A dog under 12 months of age

Purebred – A dog whose sire and dam belong to the same breed and who are of unmixed descent

Saddle – Colored markings in the shape of a saddle over the back; colors may vary

Shedding – The natural process whereby old hair falls off the dog's body as it is replaced by new hair growth.

Sire – The male parent of a dog

Smooth Coat – Short hair that is close-lying

Spay – The surgery to remove a female dog's ovaries, rendering her incapable of breeding

Trim – To groom a dog's coat by plucking or clipping

Undercoat – The soft, short coat typically concealed by a longer outer coat

Wean – The process through which puppies transition from subsisting on their mother's milk to eating solid food

Whelping – The act of birthing a litter of puppies

Chapter Two: Labradoodle Temperament Breed and Overview

Because the Labradoodle is a cross between the Poodle and the Labrador Retriever it has a very gentle temperament.

Knowing that the Labradoodle is a combination of the Labrador Retriever and Poodle breeds is not enough to truly understand this breed. Each and every dog is unique in terms of Labradoodle temperament and personality, but learning about the parent breeds will help you to understand your dog a little better. In this chapter, I will introduce you to the Labradoodle breed and provide helpful information about the parent breeds as well. You will also receive a history of the breed and an overview of different Labradoodle types and colors!

1.) *What is a Labradoodle Dog?*

You don't have to own a Labradoodle yourself in order to know what one is. These dogs are incredibly popular and for good reason! They are cute, cuddly, and absolutely full of life – you'll just have to take my word for it until you get your own. I also want to remind you that because the Labradoodle is a mixed breed dog, each one is completely unique. Dog genetics are relatively complicated so you can't expect a Labradoodle to possess all of the best traits from each parent every time. What I would recommend to you, if you want to learn more about what the Labradoodle is like, is to learn a little more about the two parent breeds – the Labrador Retriever and the Poodle. That is what you will find in this section!

a.) Labrador Retriever Breed Overview

The Labrador Retriever is consistently ranked as the most popular pure breed in the United States according to American Kennel Club (AKC) registration statistics each year. This breed is known for its friendly and fun-loving personality, but these dogs also have a bit of a mischievous side as well! Labrador Retrievers, or Labs as they are affectionately known, make excellent family pets, and they get along particularly well with children. These dogs are great companions, and they excel at dog sports too.

The Labrador Retriever is consistently ranked as the most popular dog breed in the United States.

The Labrador Retriever is a medium- to large-sized breed that generally stands between 21.5 and 24.5 inches (54 to 62 cm) tall, weighing between 55 and 80 pounds (25 to 36 kg) at maturity. Labs come in three main colors – chocolate brown, black, and golden yellow – and they generally have solid-colored coats. Their coat has a soft, insulating under layer to keep the dog warm and a harsh, protective outer layer. This type of coat is designed to protect the dog against cold water and weather while it is exercising its skills as a water retriever. Labs also have thick otter-like tails which help them to maneuver through the water.

While Labs are perfectly designed for swimming, and they are skilled retrievers, that is not all they are good for! These dogs are highly intelligent, and they respond very well to training. In fact, Labrador Retrievers are so smart that they can learn new commands with fewer than five repetitions! This breed can be trained for everything from police work and detection to search and rescue – they also make excellent service dogs and therapy dogs. In terms of dog sports, Labrador Retrievers excel in fly ball, agility, obedience, disc dog, and more.

In terms of caring for a Labrador Retriever, these dogs have relatively high energy levels, and they need a good bit of daily exercise. Not only do Labs need a lot of physical exercise to control their energy levels, but they also need plenty of mental stimulation as well. I always say that a bored Lab is a destructive Lab. When these dogs are stuck in the house all day without any attention or exercise, they have a tendency to start chewing on things, and they can become talented escape artists as well. Labrador Retrievers are certainly not a low-maintenance breed, but their wonderful personalities and other positive qualities definitely make up for that fact.

Not only are Labs friendly and wonderful pets but they are also fairly healthy as far as pure breeds go. This breed is susceptible to the same conditions you would expect to see in a large-breed dog such as hip dysplasia, gastric torsion, and obesity but they may also be prone to congenital eye conditions like cataracts and progressive retinal atrophy (PRA). Some other conditions that have been known to affect this breed include epilepsy, skin allergies, heart disease, and osteochondrosis. Some Labs also tend to develop knee problems like patellar luxation and exercise-induced collapse.

Summary of Labrador Retriever Facts

Pedigree: developed from St. John's water dogs in the Newfoundland region of Canada

AKC Group: Sporting Group

Breed Size: medium to large

Height: between 21.5 and 24.5 inches (54 to 62 cm)

Weight: between 55 and 80 pounds (25 to 36 kg)

Coat Length: short and dense

Coat Texture: double coat with fine, soft undercoat and harsh, protective outer layer

Color: chocolate brown, black or gold

Eyes and Nose: dark brown or hazel

Ears: flopped ears, soft and large

Tail: otter-tail, thick at the base and thickly furred

Temperament: friendly, gentle, people-oriented, active

Strangers: quick to make friends

Other Dogs: good with other dogs

Other Pets: generally gets along with other pets

Training: intelligent and very trainable; can learn new commands with fewer than five repetitions

Exercise Needs: fairly active or energetic; needs plenty of daily exercise and mental stimulation

Health Conditions: epilepsy, skin allergies, heart disease, osteochondrosis, hip and elbow dysplasia, gastric torsion, obesity, cataracts, progressive retinal atrophy, patellar luxation, exercise-induced collapse, etc.

Lifespan: average 12 to 13 years

b.) Poodle Breed Overview

While many people adore the Poodle for its beautifully curly coat, my favorite thing about this breed is its friendly personality and intelligence. Poodles are consistently ranked among the smartest dog breeds, and they have the potential to excel in a wide range of dog sports and working applications. Another important thing to remember about the Poodle is the fact that it comes in three different sizes – Standard, Miniature, and Toy. Each size has its own unique personality traits, so it is almost like it is three breeds in one!

The Standard Poodle is the largest of the three sizes with adult dogs standing at least 15 inches (38 cm) tall and weighing between 40 and 55 pounds (18 to 25 kg). The Toy Poodle is the smallest size, growing to a maximum height of 10 inches (25.4 cm) and weighing between 5 and 10 pounds (2.25 to 4.5 kg). The Miniature Poodle is the middle size, standing 10 to 15 inches (25.4 to 38 cm) tall and weighing 12 to 15 pounds (5.4 to 6.8 kg) on average. All three sizes have the same curly coat, but they do exhibit slightly different temperaments in some cases.

Standard Poodles are a friendly and loyal breed, forming strong bonds with family and getting along with everyone they meet. Not only does the Standard Poodle get along very well with children and other dogs but they make excellent family pets in general. This breed is very smart, so they are easy to train, and they do well in a variety of dog sports and working applications. Poodles are also a very active breed that requires plenty of daily exercise as well as mental stimulation to prevent the development of problem behavior due to boredom.

The Standard Poodle is one of the easiest breeds to identify due to its long, curly coat.

The biggest concern that most Poodle owners have is caring for their coat. The Poodle's coat is very fine and curly, but it will keep growing if you do not trim it. Most Poodle owners recommend professional grooming every 4 to 6 weeks. In the meantime, you will need to brush and comb the Poodle's coat to prevent mats and tangles. The good news is that Poodles are a low-shedding breed, so they are ideal for allergy sufferers. They do shed, but most of the shed fur gets caught in the curly coat instead of falling to the ground. You can also keep your Poodle's coat trimmed short in a puppy clip to reduce the maintenance.

When it comes to personality and temperament, there are some differences among the three sizes. All three sizes are friendly, and they make excellent companion pets, but Toy and Miniature Poodles tend to have less patience with children than Standard Poodles. Toy Poodles require a lot of attention, and they can be a little bit harder to train than the larger sizes, but they make great companion pets. The Miniature Poodle is the most active of the three sizes, and they are relatively mischievous as well. Standard Poodles are the most reserved and gentle of the three sizes, and they are the best with children.

As smart as Poodles are, they can become a little bit stubborn at times. Plenty of socialization and training is recommended for this breed, especially if you plan to train your Poodle for dog sports or various working applications. The Toy and Miniature Poodles might take a little longer to housetrain, and you might need to be a little bit firmer with your discipline in order to discourage undesired behaviors. Despite all of these things, however, the Poodle makes an excellent family pet in all three sizes.

In terms of their health, Poodles are a relatively long-lived breed with an average lifespan across all three sizes of 14 to 18 years. The Standard Poodle is affected by a number of conditions including Addison's disease, Cushing's syndrome, hypothyroidism, and progressive retinal atrophy. Toy Poodles, in particular, are prone to Legg-Calve-Perthes disease as well as dental problems. All three sizes are prone to skin problems and food allergies as well as epilepsy and certain kinds of cancer.

Summary of Poodle Breed Info

Pedigree: developed from various water retrievers in Germany; smaller sizes were selectively bred for size

AKC Group: Non-Sporting Group

Breed Size: small, medium, large

Height: over 15 inches (38 cm) Standard; between 10 and 15 inches (24.5 to 38 cm) Miniature; at or under 10 inches (24.5 cm) Toy

Weight: 40 to 55 pounds (18 to 25 kg) Standard; 12 to 15 pounds (5.4 to 6.8 kg) Miniature; 5 to 10 pounds (2.25 to 4.5 kg) Toy Poodle

Coat Length: medium to long

Coat Texture: fine and curly; single layer

Color: white, brown, black, silver, gray, beige, apricot, red, cream sable; solid, parti-color, bi-color, phantom, or brindle patterns allowed

Eyes and Nose: dark brown or black

Ears: flopped ears, well covered in fur

Tail: generally carried high

Temperament: friendly, lively, people-oriented, active

Strangers: may be shy around strangers but warms up quickly once introduced

Other Dogs: generally good with other dogs

Other Pets: generally gets along with other pets

Training: intelligent and very trainable; Toy and Miniature sizes may take longer to housetrain than other dogs

Exercise Needs: fairly active or energetic; needs plenty of daily exercise and mental stimulation

Health Conditions: Addison's disease, Cushing's syndrome, hypothyroidism, progressive retinal atrophy, dental problems, skin problems, food allergies, etc.

Lifespan: average 14 to 18 years

2.) *Labradoodle Information and Facts*

Labradoodles are a people-oriented breed with a bit of a goofy side
– they love to run and play with their human companions!

Now that you've been introduced to the two parent breeds, you should have a better idea of what the Labradoodle is like. As I have already mentioned, it is impossible to predict exactly what a designer dog will be like due to the complexity of genetics, but you can make certain predictions about the Labradoodle breed as a whole. For example, because both the Poodle and the Labrador Retriever are friendly, social breeds you can expect the same from your Labradoodle!

The typical temperament of the Labradoodle breed as a whole is friendly and people-oriented, sometimes with a bit of a goofy side. Labradoodles tend to make friends very quickly which is why they generally don't do well as guard dogs – they are more likely to greet a stranger with a wagging tail than to sound the alarm. It depends, of course, on which type of Poodle is used in the crossing because Standard Poodles tend to be a little more reserved around strangers until they get to know them.

In terms of appearance, you can expect the Labradoodle to have a wavy or curly coat. The actual texture of the dog's coat can vary from soft and fine to somewhat wiry. It is possible for a Labradoodle's coat to be straight, though most dogs of this breed have some degree of wave or curl to their coats. Many Labradoodle breeders describe straight-coated dogs as having hair coats while curly-coated dogs have wool coats, and wavy-coated dogs have fleece coats. Due to their Poodle heritage, Labradoodles tend to shed less than Labrador Retrievers, but they are not an entirely non-shedding breed. They may be a good choice for allergy sufferers, however, especially if you brush and bathe your dog regularly.

Labradoodle dogs come in a wide variety of different colors. While Labrador Retrievers are usually solid-colored with either black, yellow, or brown coats, Poodles come in all colors and patterns. It is not uncommon for Labradoodles to have particolored coats like a Poodle, but it is more common for them to have solid-colored coats with some variation in the color on their ears, face, feet, and tails. Labradoodles come in all colors including white, peach, cream, apricot, gold, tan, brown, beige, red, black, silver, and nearly any other color you can imagine.

In the same way that the color and coat of the Labradoodle vary widely from one dog to another, so can the size. I have found it to be true with any designer dog that it is impossible to predict the size of the adult dog based on the size of the puppy. This is particularly the case for Labradoodles since Poodles themselves come in three sizes. It stands to reason that Labradoodles bred from Standard Poodles will be larger than those bred from Toy or Miniature Poodles, but there is still a great deal of variation. I will go more into detail about the different Labradoodle sizes later in this chapter.

When it comes to Labradoodle temperament, these dogs are always friendly and sociable, though individual personalities may vary. My oldest Labradoodle Sandy, for example, is very outgoing, and he would spend all day running around in the yard if he could. My younger one, Layla, is still incredibly gentle and good with people, but she is a little more mild-mannered. She would rather hang back and play with her favorite chew toy than go tearing around the yard like Sandy. You won't really be able to know what your Labradoodle puppy's personality will be like until he grows up.

Though you can't predict exactly what your Labradoodle will be like most dogs of this breed are excellent family pets. They are very patient and gentle with children (though this may be a little less true with Labradoodles bred from Toy or Miniature Poodles). They love to spend time with family, and they are incredibly loyal. This breed tends to get along well with other dogs, and they also do well with cats and other household pets, particularly if they are raised with them from a young age. Socialization and training are necessary for Labradoodles, though this applies to all dogs.

In terms of energy levels and exercise requirements, Labradoodles can be a little bit high-maintenance. The Lab side of this breed has boundless energy and a good bit of mischievousness. The Poodle side is just as active but generally a little bit easier to control. Labradoodles need a good 30-minute walk once-a-day, and they will appreciate some active playtime at home or in the backyard. It is also a good idea to give your Labradoodle plenty of mental stimulation on a daily basis using interactive toys or training games to keep his mind sharp. As I have already said, a bored dog is a destructive dog, and intelligent breeds like the Labradoodle are especially prone to destructive habits if they don't get enough exercise or attention on a daily basis.

Like the size and personality of this breed, the health of the Labradoodle is also somewhat difficult to predict. The average lifespan for the breed is around 10 to 15 years, though breeding will play a significant role in determining your dog's life expectancy. As a medium- to large-sized breed, the Labradoodle is prone to certain musculoskeletal issues such as elbow and hip dysplasia as well as gastric torsion. These dogs have been known to develop skin and food allergies as well as recurrent ear infections. Labradoodles inherit the risk for Cushing's syndrome and Addison's disease from their Poodle side and a risk for congenital eye conditions from their Lab side. Other diseases known to affect the breed include epilepsy, diabetes, hypothyroidism and von Willebrand's disease.

Summary of Labradoodle Facts

Pedigree: cross between the Labrador Retriever and the Poodle (any of the three sizes)

AKC Group: not AKC-recognized

Breed Size: miniature, medium, and standard

Height: 14 to 16 inches (35.5 to 40.6 cm) Miniature; 17 to 20 inches (43.2 to 50.8 cm) Medium; 21 to 24 inches (53.5 to 61 cm) Standard

Weight: 15 to 25 pounds (6.8 to 11.3 kg) Miniature; 30 to 45 pounds (13.6 to 20.4 kg) Medium; 50 to 65 pounds (22.7 to 29.5 kg) Standard

Coat Length: short, medium, or long

Coat Texture: fine, wool, or fleece

Color: any color including white, peach, cream, apricot, gold, tan, brown, beige, red, black, silver; solid, parti-color, or bi-color

Eyes and Nose: dark brown or black

Ears: flopped ears, well covered in fur

Tail: generally carried high

Temperament: friendly, lively, people-oriented, active

Strangers: may be shy around strangers but warms up quickly once introduced

Other Dogs: generally good with other dogs

Other Pets: generally gets along with other pets

Training: intelligent and very trainable; Miniature size may take longer to housetrain than other dogs

Exercise Needs: fairly active or energetic; needs plenty of daily exercise and mental stimulation

Health Conditions: Addison's disease, Cushing's syndrome, hypothyroidism, progressive retinal atrophy, skin problems, food allergies, hip dysplasia, elbow dysplasia, ear infections, diabetes, etc.

Lifespan: average 10 to 15 years

3.) *Labradoodle Breed History*

The name Labradoodle first appeared during the mid-1950s, but it wasn't popularized until several decades later. The breeder who is credited with actually developing the Labradoodle breed is Wally Conron, an Australian breeder who worked with the Royal Guide Dogs Association of Australia. Conron made it his goal to create a breed that combined the low-shedding coat of the Poodle with the intelligence, gentleness, and trainability of the Labrador Retriever. This dog was meant to serve as a guide dog for people who had allergies to dogs.

One of the first puppies from Conron's breeding program that showed these characteristics was Sultan – this dog ended up serving as a guide dog for a woman in Hawaii for a decade. This dog set the stage for other assistance and guide dog organizations in Australia and around the world to add Labradoodles to their training programs. Today, the Labradoodle is known not only for its talent as a guide dog and assistance dog but also for its calm, gentle temperament which makes it the perfect family pet and companion.

4.) Labradoodle Types and Sizes

The Labrador Retriever comes in three main colors – these are some of the most common colors seen in Labradoodles as well.

Because there are different kinds of Poodles and Labrador Retrievers, it only stands to reason that there will be different Labradoodle types and sizes as well.

a.) American Labradoodle

The American Labradoodle is another name for the standard Labradoodle-type dog bred from a Poodle and a Labrador Retriever in the United States. These dogs do not necessarily have to be a 50-50 cross of Poodle and Lab blood; the Labradoodle can also be bred from the offspring resulting from the first-generation crossing of a Poodle and Labrador Retriever.

b.) Australian Labradoodle

The Australian Labradoodle is very similar to the American Labradoodle in many ways, but there may be more than just Poodle and Labrador Retriever genes used in the crossing. Australian breeders Tegan Park and Rutland Manor are generally credited with developing the Australian Labradoodle breed and, in addition to the Poodle and Labrador Retriever genetics, some of the other breeds used in the development may include the following:

- Irish Water Spaniel
- Curly Coat Retriever
- American Cocker Spaniel
- English Cocker Spaniel

Because the Australian Labradoodle has not been recognized as a separate breed there is no set breed standard – it is entirely possible that Australian Labradoodle dogs exist with other breeds used in their pedigree. Australian Labradoodles still come in different sizes depending on the type of Poodle used, though the standards seem to differentiate between two sizes rather than three – there is a Standard Australian Labradoodle and a Miniature Australian Labradoodle.

c.) Standard Labradoodle

The Standard Labradoodle is the most common size, and it comes from the crossing of a Labrador Retriever with a Standard Poodle. The average size range for a female Standard Labradoodle is between 21 and 23 inches (53.3 to 58.4 cm) and, for a male, it is 22 to 24 inches (55.9 to 61 cm). Both sexes reach a mature weight of between 50 and 65 pounds (22.7 to 39.5 kg) in most cases.

d.) Mini Labradoodle or Miniature Labradoodle

The middle size for the Labradoodle is called by a number of different names depending whom you talk to. The name I hear most often is Medium Labradoodle, though they are also known as Mini Labradoodle or Miniature Labradoodle. The Medium Labradoodle is bred from the Labrador Retriever and a Miniature Poodle, which is the middle size. These dogs generally weigh 30 to 45 pounds (13.6 to 20.4 kg) at maturity with females standing 17 to 19 inches (43.2 to 48.3 cm) tall and males reaching 18 to 20 inches (45.7 to 50.8 cm).

e.) Toy Labradoodle or Small Labradoodle

The smallest Labradoodle size is the Toy Labradoodle or Small Labradoodle, though I generally use the term Miniature Labradoodle for the smallest size. These dogs are bred from Labrador Retrievers and Toy Poodles, the smallest of the three sizes. This size of Labradoodle weighs 15 to 25 pounds (6.8 to 11.3 kg) on average and stands somewhere between 14 and 16 inches (35.6 to 40.6 cm) tall at maturity.

5.) *Labradoodle Dog Colors and Pictures of Labradoodles*

I love my Labradoodle's energy and friendly personality, but I also love the way he looks. There is just something about that fluffy, curly coat that begs to be stroked! What I love about Labradoodles is the fact that they come in so many different colors, and each one is more beautiful than the last. In this section, you'll find a quick description of the different Labradoodle dog colors so you can start thinking about which one might be the right choice for your own Labradoodle.

a.) Chocolate Labradoodle

One of the most popular Labradoodle colors is the chocolate Labradoodle. These dogs inherit their color from the chocolate brown Labrador Retriever and a brown

Poodle. The shade of brown ranges from a light brown to a deep chocolate brown, depending on the breeding.

b.) Black Labradoodle

Another one of the most common Labradoodle colors is the black Labradoodle. These dogs inherit their color from the black Labrador Retriever and a black or dark-colored Poodle. Black Labradoodles not only have black fur, but they also have black eyelids, lips, noses, and pads.

c.) Golden Labradoodle

The golden Labradoodle inherits its color from the yellow Labrador Retriever and a light-colored

Poodle. The actual shade of gold may vary from a light cream color to a lovely golden yellow.

d.) Red Labradoodle

The red Labradoodle inherits most of its red color from the Poodle side of its genetics, though there is a fox red variety of Labrador Retriever, which is less common than the main three colors. Red Labradoodles may vary in shade from a light reddish-brown to a deep mahogany red.

e.) White Labradoodle

The white Labradoodle inherits its color from a yellow Labrador Retriever and a white or light-colored Poodle. While white Poodles are a solid, bright white, the white Labradoodle may have hints of cream, silver or gray in its coat. White Labradoodles generally still have dark eyes, noses, and pads.

f.) Apricot Labradoodle

 Apricot is a color seen in the Poodle breed which is a light cream color with just a hint of red. Apricot Labradoodles are generally bred from light-colored yellow Labrador Retrievers and red or apricot Poodles.

Chapter Three: Labrador Poodle Information

Many Labradoodle owners say that the breed combines the best qualities of both parent breeds – what do you think?

As much as I adore my Labradoodles, I have to admit that they do require a certain degree of work to maintain. I assure you, however, that it is all worth it! Before you go and get a Labradoodle puppy of your own, however, I want to make sure that you understand some of the most practical aspects of owning a Labrador Poodle. In this chapter, you will learn the rules for licensing your dog as well as the pros and cons for the breed. I'll also go into details about what kind of costs you can expect if you become a Labradoodle owner.

1.) Do You Need a License?

Before you bring home a new pet – whether it be a dog or something else - it is always a good idea to check your regional or local requirements for licensing and permits. The licensing requirements for pets including dogs are different in the various countries, and even in different states, so be careful. Even if your state doesn't mandate that you have to license your Labradoodle, it might still be a good idea. When you license your dog, he will be assigned a specific license number that will be associated with your contact information – if he gets lost and someone finds him, he or she may be able to contact you using the information from the license.

In the United States, it is true that there are no federal licensing requirements for dogs, but that simply means that these things are determined at the state level instead. Most states do require dog owners to license their dogs, and the licenses are generally renewable annually. Dog licenses in the United States only cost about $25 (£22.50), and they must be paired with an updated rabies vaccination – each year you will have to renew the license and prove that your dog is current on his rabies vaccine as well. When you get your Labradoodle vaccinated your vet will provide you with a rabies tag and a number to give as proof when applying for your dog license.

The licensing requirements for dogs in the United Kingdom and in other parts of Europe are a little bit different than in the U.S. The United Kingdom makes it mandatory for all dog owners to license their dogs and the cost is similar to the expense of a dog license in the U.S. One major difference you should keep in mind, however, is that dogs in the U.K. do not need to be vaccinated against rabies because the virus has been eradicated in the U.K. If you plan to move your dog into or out of the country, however, you will need to obtain an Animal Movement License (AML) to make sure your dog doesn't contract or spread any diseases during his travel. Pets are also subject to a quarantine period before and after travel.

2.) Do Labradoodles Get Along with Other Pets?

The Labradoodle is a very people-oriented breed, but they also tend to get along well with other dogs and household pets.

The Labradoodle is a very social breed that tends to make friends with everyone it meets – this often applies to dogs and other animals. For the most part, Labradoodles do get along very well with other dogs, and they can even do well with cats and other household pets. To ensure that your Labradoodle gets along with other pets, it is best to raise them together from a young age. You should always supervise early interactions until you know how your pets will react to each other. Even after they get used to each other, you should still be careful just in case.

3.) *How Many Labradoodles Should You Get?*

This is one of the questions I hear most often when it comes to new dog owners and, unfortunately, the answer is not as straightforward as you might like because there are multiple factors to consider. For one thing, you have to consider that the Labradoodle is a very social breed that needs a lot of daily exercise and attention. These dogs do not do well when left alone for extended periods of time so, if you work a full-time job or leave the house for hours at a time, you may want a second Labradoodle (or another dog) to keep your dog company. You also have to consider, however, the added cost and time commitment to care for a second dog. If you are worried about your Labradoodle getting enough attention, but you can't afford a second dog, consider hiring a dog walker or pet sitter instead.

4.) Labradoodle Prices and Costs

The average cost for a Labradoodle puppy varies widely depending on the quality of the breeding stock and other factors.

There is no denying that dogs can be expensive, especially if you are willing to do what it takes to keep your dog in the best of health. Not only do you have to worry about the purchase price for your Labradoodle puppy but you also have to factor in recurring costs for food, veterinary care, vaccinations, and more. In this section, I'm going to provide you an overview of the expenses associated with bringing your Labradoodle puppy home for the first time (your initial expenditure) as well as the monthly costs you should come to expect.

a.) Initial Costs for Labradoodle Puppies

The initial costs for keeping a Labradoodle dog include the price to purchase your puppy (or to adopt an adult Labradoodle), the cost of a crate and/or dog bed, food and water bowls, toys and accessories, microchipping, vaccinations, spay/neuter surgery, and grooming supplies. <u>You will find an overview of each of these costs as well as an estimate for each cost below</u>:

Labradoodle Dog Price – The average price Labradoodle puppy breeders charge can vary widely depending on a number of factors. For one thing, the cost to purchase and raise a Standard Poodle is different from that of a Miniature or Toy Poodle, so those costs will be factored in. It is also true that pure breeds like the Lab and the Poodle come in different qualities – pet-quality dogs are less expensive than show-quality dogs.

The minimum you should expect to pay for Labradoodle puppies is about $750 (£518), but you shouldn't be surprised to see prices as high as $2,500 (£1,725). Just be careful when shopping for Labradoodle breeders to make sure you aren't taken advantage of by a hobby breeder – if you pay a high price for your Labradoodle you should make sure that it is bred from high-quality parents. If you chose to get your dog from a Labradoodle rescue, the cost of Labradoodle adoption is usually under $300 (£207).

Crate and/or Dog Bed – When you start training your Labradoodle puppy you will want to have a crate that you can keep him in overnight and when you are away from home. To make your dog's crate more comfortable, you should line it with a blanket or dog bed. The average cost for these things together is around $50 (£34.50).

Food/Water Bowls – Buying quality food and water bowls for your dog is important because he will use them every day. Your best option is stainless steel because it is easy to clean and doesn't harbor bacteria – ceramic is another good choice . The average costs for a quality set of stainless steel bowls are about $20 (£13.80).

Toys and Accessories – In addition to food and water bowls, your Labradoodle will also need certain accessories like chew toys, a collar, a leash, and perhaps a harness. The cost for these items varies depending on quality, but you should budget about $50 (£34.50) for all of these costs combined.

Microchipping – Having your Labradoodle microchipped is not a requirement, but it is a great idea – I have all of my dog's microchipped for their own protection in case they get lost. A microchip is similar to a license in that it comes with a number that is correlated with your contact information. The difference is that the microchip is implanted under your dog's skin so it cannot be lost. The procedure only takes a few minutes, and it doesn't hurt your dog – plus, it only costs about $30 (£20.75) if you go to a clinic or shelter.

Vaccinations – Immediately after Labradoodle puppies are born they drink their mother's milk which contains antibodies to protect them until their immune systems develop. During the first year, you will also need to make sure your Labradoodle puppy gets certain vaccines to protect him against disease. Depending what Labradoodle breeder you get your puppy from, he may already have one or more vaccinations under his belt. Still, you should budget a cost of about $50 (£34.50) for initial vaccinations.

Spay/Neuter Surgery – If you do not plan to breed your Labradoodle (and you should carefully think before you do), you should have your dog altered before 6 months of age. If you go to a veterinary surgeon, this procedure could cost you hundreds of dollars, but you can save money by going to a vet clinic. The average clinic cost for spay surgery is $100 to $200 (£69 - £138), and the average cost for neuter surgery is around $50 to $100 (£34.50 - £69).

Grooming Supplies – Labradoodles come with all kinds of coats so the grooming supplies you need will vary depending on the type of coat your dog has. In order to keep your dog's coat healthy and tangle-free, however, you'll want to brush and comb it several times a week. You may also want to trim the fur between your dog's toes once a week. For grooming supplies, you will need a wide-toothed comb, a wire-pin brush, some dog shampoo, and a set of nail clippers. The cost for these supplies varies depending on quality, but you should set aside $50 (£34.50) to be safe.

To put all of this information together in your head, here is a chart detailing the costs for one Labradoodle and for two Labradoodle dogs as well as a total cost at the end:

Initial Costs for Labradoodle Dogs		
Cost	**One Dog**	**Two Dogs**
Labradoodle Price	$300 to $2,500 (£207 - £1,725)	$600 to $5,000 (£415 - £3,450)
Crate/Bed	$50 (£34.50)	$100 (£69)

Food/Water Bowls	$20 (£13.80)	$40 (£27.65)
Toys/Accessories	$50 (£34.50)	$100 (£69)
Microchipping	$30 (£20.75)	$60 (£41.50)
Vaccinations	$50 (£34.50)	$100 (£69)
Spay/Neuter	$50 to $200 (£34.50 - £138)	$100 to $400 (£69 - £277)
Grooming Supplies	$50 (£34.50)	$50 (£34.50)
Total	$600 to $2,900 (£415 – £2,001)	$1,150 to $5,850 (£795 – £4,037)

*Prices may vary by region and are subject to change.

**Prices are calculated based on the exchange rate of $1 = £0.69

b.) Monthly Costs for Adult Labradoodles

The monthly costs for keeping a Labradoodle dog as a pet include all of the recurring costs you need to cover on a monthly or yearly basis. These costs may include the cost of food and treats, veterinary care, license renewal, grooming costs, and others. <u>You will find an overview of each of these expenses as well as an estimate for each of these costs below</u>:

Food and Treats – Because the Labradoodle is a medium- to large-sized breed, your monthly costs for food will not be insubstantial. You can expect to spend about $35 (£24.15) on a large bag of high-quality dog food that will last you about 4 to 6 weeks.

Veterinary Care – Once your Labradoodle puppy gets all the shots he needs during his first year, you will only need to take him to the vet once or twice a year for check-ups. The average cost for a vet check-up for a dog is about $40 (£27.65). If you have two vet visits per year and divide that total cost over 12 months, you will get a monthly cost around $7 (£4.80).

License Renewal – Renewing your Labradoodle dog's license each year will not be a major expense – it should only cost you about $25 (£17.30). If you divide that cost over twelve months, you have a monthly cost of $2 (£1.40).

Grooming – One of your biggest monthly costs for your dog is going to be Labradoodle grooming. You'll need to brush your dog's coat daily yourself but should also have your dog professionally groomed several times per year; most owners recommend grooming every 3 months. A single grooming visit for a Poodle costs about $50 (£34.50) so plan to spend at least this much every 3 months or more on your Labradoodle dog – this gives you an average monthly cost of $17 (£11.75).

Other Costs – In addition to the costs that have already been mentioned, you may find yourself dealing with unexpected costs for the replacement of toys and food bowls, or you might need to replace your dog's collar. These costs will not occur every month, but you should set aside about $10 (£6.90) each month to be prepared.

To put all of this information together in your head, here is a chart detailing the costs for one Labradoodle and for two Labradoodle dogs as well as a total cost at the end:

Monthly Costs for Labradoodle Dogs		
Cost	One Dog	Two Dogs
Food and Treats	$35 (£24.15)	$70 (£48.30)
Vet Care	$7 (£4.80)	$14 (£9.70)
License Renewal	$2 (£1.40)	$4 (£2.75)
Grooming	$17 (£11.75)	$34 (£23.50)
Other Costs	$10 (£6.90)	$20 (£13.80)
Total	$71 (£49)	$142 (£98)

*Prices may vary by region and are subject to change.
**Prices are calculated based on the exchange rate of $1 = £0.69

5.) *Labrador Poodle Pros and Cons*

It doesn't matter what kind of pet you are thinking about getting, it is always a good idea to learn about the good AND the bad things. By now you've heard me say a thousand times that Labradoodles are an amazing breed, but even I can admit that they aren't the right dog breed for everyone. Before you go out and buy a Labradoodle puppy, I want to make sure that you understand the pros and cons of the breed. You'll find an overview of Labrador Poodle pros and cons in this section:

Pros for Labradoodles

- Labradoodles are a friendly and gentle breed, usually mild-mannered and sociable.
- These dogs are patient with children and make excellent family pets.
- Labradoodles generally get along with other dogs and various household pets when raised together.
- This breed comes in a wide variety of colors and patterns, and they are very beautiful.
- Labradoodles are highly intelligent, and they generally respond well to training – they can also be trained for competition and various dog sports.

- This breed has a low-shedding coat which makes it easy to maintain and ideal for allergy sufferers.

Cons for Labradoodles

- The Labradoodle is a fairly active and energetic breed that needs plenty of daily exercise.
- Labradoodles do not do well when left alone for extended periods of time – they need human companionship and lots of daily attention.
- Though their coat is low-shedding, it does grow quickly, so they need plenty of regular brushing and grooming.
- Labradoodles are very smart which means that they tend to get into trouble, especially if they get bored.
- This breed can grow fairly large depending on breeding, so they need a lot of space and a decent amount of food.
- Labradoodles are prone to some serious health problems, so DNA testing and responsible breeding is a must.

Chapter Four: Where to Find Labradoodle Breeders and Labradoodle Puppies for Sale

To make sure that you get to enjoy your Labradoodle's company for as long as possible, start with a healthy, well-bred puppy.

When you decide to get a new puppy it is easy to get caught up in the excitement – trust me, I've been there. But I want you to know how important it is to exercise caution at this point. Do not rush out and buy the first Labradoodle puppy you find. If you want to make sure that the puppy you bring home is healthy and well-bred you need to take your time in researching and choosing a responsible breeder. In this chapter, I'm going to tell you what you need to do to find one of these breeders, and I'll give you tips for picking a healthy puppy.

1.) *Where to Look for American Labradoodle Breeders*

Once you determine that the Labradoodle is the right breed for you, you may think that the next step is to head to your local pet store to buy one. This is what many inexperienced dog owners assume to be the best option for finding a puppy, but I want to caution you against this. While some pet stores get their dogs from local rescue groups, many of them source their puppies from puppy mills – you absolutely do not want a puppy mill puppy. A puppy mill is a breeding operation that puts profit over the welfare of the dogs. They force dogs to reproduce litter after litter with minimal veterinary care, keeping them in squalid conditions.

Puppy mills do not screen their breeding stock to minimize the risk of passing on genetic conditions which means that the puppies have an increased likelihood of inheriting those conditions. This is especially dangerous for a breed like the Labradoodle where the two parent breeds are prone to multiple congenital conditions – if the two parents carry genes for the same disease, the chances of the puppy getting it are much higher. This is why responsible breeders DNA-test their breeding stock.

Instead of purchasing a puppy from a pet store, you should take the time to find an experienced Labradoodle breeder. You can start with an online search to find breeders in your region, but you may also be able to get some personal recommendations from a local vet clinic or rescue group. Put together a list of several breeders and then take the time to vet them thoroughly in order to determine whether they are responsible, experienced, and worth buying a puppy from.

Here is a step-by-step guide for vetting a Labradoodle breeder:

- Gather contact information and take the time to visit the website for each breeder on your list.
  - Read the information provided on the website about the breeder to help determine whether they are a legitimate operation or just a backyard breeder.
  - Look for red flags like extremely high Labradoodle prices, lack of breed club registration, no information about the breeding stock, etc.
- Narrow down your list of breeders, eliminating any that seem to be irresponsible or hobby breeders based on your review of their websites.
- Contact the remaining breeders on your list and schedule a face-to-face interview, is possible.

- o Ask the breeder detailed questions about the breeding operation including his experience with dog breeding in general and with the dog breed Labradoodle in particular – the breeder should also know a great deal about the Poodle and the Labrador Retriever.
- o Ask about the pedigree and health status of the breeding stock for whatever litters are available – it is a red flag if the breeder won't give you this information.
- o Ask about the policy for reserving a puppy – a reputable breeder won't let you purchase a puppy outright without meeting you, and he will be just as eager to ask you questions as you are to ask him in order to ensure that you will give the puppy a good home.

- After speaking to the breeders over the phone or in person, ask for a tour of the breeding facilities.
  - o Make sure to view the facilities where the breeding stock is kept in addition to where the puppies are being kept.
  - o Ensure that the facilities are clean and well-kept – if the place is dirty or if there are signs of diarrhea, avoid purchasing from that breeder.
  - o Make sure that the breeding stock is in good health and that the dogs are a good example of

the breed standard – view the pedigrees and
health certificates for the dogs, if possible.

o   Consider it a red flag if the breeder is not willing
to show you the facilities and the breeding stock.

After you have taken the time to narrow down your
list of breeders to just one or two options, you will have a
pretty good idea what you are getting yourself into, but you
should still be careful about the process of selecting your
puppy. I will go into this process in greater detail later in
this chapter.

2.) Where to Find Australian Labradoodle Breeders and Australian Labradoodle Puppies

Australian Labradoodles are a little bit different from American Labradoodles because they have a mixed pedigree but both types are equally beautiful!

There are two different kinds of Australian Labradoodles – those that are bred in the United States and those that are bred in Australia. As I already explained earlier in this book, Australian Labradoodles sometimes have different breeds mixed into their pedigree besides just the Labrador Retriever and the Poodle. This is why you need to be especially careful when choosing Australian

Labradoodle breeders. Different breeders might follow a different standard, so do your research to make sure that you get exactly what you want.

If you want an Australian Labradoodle, you will need first to decide whether you want to buy one bred in the United States or in Australia. If you purchase a puppy from Australia, you may need to pay to have the puppy shipped – this comes with its own unique set of challenges. For one thing, you may not be able actually to see or interact with the puppy before you purchase it. The breeder might give you pictures of the puppy, but you do not have a guarantee that the puppy you see in pictures is the puppy you actually get – there are lots of risks involved with purchasing puppies and having them shipped overseas.

You should still follow the recommendations from the previous section to select a responsible Australian Labradoodle breeder to reduce the risk that you end up with a poorly bred puppy. In addition to following these general guidelines, however, you'll need to ask the breeder some additional questions. What breed standard does the breeder follow and what other breeds are used in the pedigree for his Labradoodles? Not only should you find out what other breeds are used in the crossing, but you should also ask why the breeder included them – it may be to achieve a particular type of coat or for certain temperament or personality traits. Get as much information from the breeder as you can before you commit.

3.) *How to Pick a Healthy Labradoodle Puppy*

If you are fortunate enough to find a Labradoodle breeder who lives close enough for you to make a visit you should definitely take the trip to pick out your own puppy. You've already gone through the process of narrowing down your list of breeders to the best option, and you should use a similar process to choose the specific puppy that you want. The more careful you are in selecting your puppy, the lower the risk that you end up with a puppy who is poorly bred or already sick.

Here are my recommendations for what to do when you get to the breeder to pick out your puppy:

- Observe the puppies to see how they interact with each other before you try to interact with them – make sure that they are active and playful, not lethargic or depressed.
- See how the puppies respond to your presence – they may be a little wary around strangers, but they should not be overly frightened. They should get over their nervousness quickly and show curiosity about you.
- Kneel down and let the Labradoodle puppies approach you when they are ready.

- Interact with the puppies a little bit by petting them gently and speaking to them, making sure that they have a positive response.
  - Pick up the puppies one by one to gauge their temperaments and to check for physical signs of illness or injury.
- Examine the puppies one-by-one to make sure they all seem to be in good health and condition. A healthy puppy will display the following signs:
  - Clear, bright eyes with no sign of discharge.
  - Clean ears – no redness, swelling, or odor.
  - No sign of diarrhea under the tail.
  - Clean, soft fur with no patches missing, even in texture.
  - No bumps or wounds on the body.
  - Healthy activity and sound movement.
- Ask the breeder for the vet and medical information for whatever puppy you are considering to confirm that it is in good health.
- If you strike a bond with one of the puppies and are able to determine that it is in good health, you can ask the breeder about the process of putting down a deposit.

It is important to remember that a responsible breeder won't send a puppy home with his new owner until he is at least 8 weeks old – 12 weeks is generally better.

Unless the puppy is fully weaned and functioning independently of his mother, you shouldn't take it home quite yet.

a.) Precautions for Miniature Labradoodle Puppies for Sale

While it is important to be careful when selecting a Labradoodle puppy, there are some extra precautions you should take when shopping for Miniature Labradoodle puppies. Early on in this book, I told you that it is impossible to predict the adult size of a Labradoodle based on its size as a puppy. This being the case, you can see how there might be an added degree of risk when it comes to purchasing a Miniature Labradoodle puppy – you have no way of knowing that the puppy you are buying will actually grow to the average miniature size, not larger.

One way to reduce your risk in this area is to pay a visit to the breeder before you commit to buying a puppy. Make sure the breeder shows you the two dogs that were used in the crossing – the Poodle half of the pair should be either a Miniature Poodle or a Toy Poodle. Remember, Miniature Poodles are a little bit bigger than Toy Poodles so if small size is important to you then pick a breeder that uses a Toy Poodle.

Some Labradoodle breeders also select their Labrador Retrievers carefully to reduce the size of the offspring. Like any breed, Labrador Retrievers can be selectively bred for size, but they are still a medium- to large-sized breed. Female Labs tend to be a little smaller than males, so using a female Lab and a male Poodle in the crossing may help to keep the puppies small. In the end, however, you won't know the maximum size your Miniature Labradoodle will reach until he actually gets there. You'll just have to take the breeder's word for it and hope that you get what you want.

4.) *Pros and Cons of Labradoodle Adoption*

If you don't feel up to the task of raising a Labradoodle puppy, consider adopting an adult dog – shelter dogs make great pets!

While there is nothing cuter than a cuddly Labradoodle puppy I have to admit that these dogs are quite the handful when they are young. If you bring home a puppy you not only have to commit to socializing and housebreaking him, but you also have to make sure he gets his initial vaccinations, and you have to deal with the consequences of the "puppy phase" (I have lost many a shoe to the puppy phase!). If you don't like the sound of these added responsibilities, you have another option –

adopting an adult Labradoodle. Below I have compiled a list of pros and cons for Labradoodle adoption that you should consider before you automatically assume your only option is to buy a puppy.

Pros for Labradoodle Adoption

- You will have peace of mind in knowing that you saved a life – you gave a home to a homeless dog.
- The dog you bring home will likely already be housetrained, so you don't have to do that yourself!
- Many adult dogs available for adoption already have some degree of obedience training under their belt.
- Adopting an adult Labradoodle means that you don't have to guess at his adult size – you can see it.
- Adult dogs already have their personalities developed so you can see whether you get along with the dog.
- Dog adoption is much more affordable than buying a puppy in most cases, and the dog will likely already be spayed/neutered and be up to date on shots.

Cons for Labradoodle Adoption

- You may not have as many options to choose from in terms of color or pattern for the dog.

- Labradoodles are a very popular breed, so they tend to go quickly in rescues – you may need to travel to find one.
- The Labradoodle you adopt may already have some behavioral problems that you might need to deal with.
- Some dogs simply don't adjust well to shelter life so the personality of the dog you see in the shelter may be more subdued than the one you see once your dog gets used to his new home.
- Many dogs that enter the shelter system are abandoned which means that there may not be any medical history available for them.

These are just a few of the pros and cons you should consider before deciding to adopt a Labradoodle rescue dog. If you do choose to adopt, be careful about which rescue group you choose and learn as much as you can about the dog before you commit to adoption.

a.) Where to Find Labradoodle Rescues and Labradoodles for Adoption

If you think that adopting an adult Labradoodle might be the right option for you, take the time to do your research and find a Labradoodle rescue group. If you cannot find a dedicated Labradoodle rescue in your area, you may still be able to find Labradoodles for adoption at your local humane society or another rescue group.

To help you find adoptable Labradoodles, try the following organizations:

United States Labradoodle Rescues

International Doodle Owners Group Rescue.
http://idogrescue.com/

Doodle Trust Rescue. http://www.doodletrust.com/

Poo-Mix Rescue. http://poomixrescue.com/

Doodle Rescue Collective, Inc. http://doodlerescue.org/

Australian Labradoodle Association of America.
https://alaa-labradoodles.com/

United Kingdom Dog Rescues

The United Kingdom does not have as many dedicated Labradoodle rescue groups, but you may be able to find Labradoodles for adoption at the following organizations:

Doodle Dogs. http://doodlerescue.org/

Last Chance Animal Rescue.
http://www.lastchanceanimalrescue.co.uk/

West Yorkshire Dog Rescue.
http://www.westyorkshiredogrescue.co.uk/

Waggy Tails Rescue. http://www.waggytails.org.uk/

The U.K. Labradoodle Association.
http://www.labradoodle.org.uk/

Chapter Five: Labradoodle Dog Care Guide

The Labradoodle is by no means a high-maintenance breed but owning a dog is a big responsibility no matter what breed it is.

From the moment you bring your Labradoodle home, he becomes your responsibility. As much as I love being a dog owner, I sometimes have to remind myself that it isn't all fun and games – I also have to pay attention to my Labradoodle's needs to make sure they are being met. In this chapter, I will give you an overview of everything you need to know about your Labradoodle's home requirements, nutritional requirements and grooming needs. All three of these things are incredibly important!

1.) *Labradoodle Home Requirements*

When it comes to caring for the Labradoodle, I want you to know that this is not a high-maintenance breed. That being said, there are still certain requirements your dog has that you are responsible for meeting. For example, all dogs need a certain amount of daily exercise, and they do best in certain housing situations. One of the things I love about the Labradoodle is the fact that they are a highly adaptable breed. They are not overly active, but they do require a good bit of exercise. As long as you meet your dog's needs for exercise and activity, however, these dogs can be adaptable to a variety of living situations.

a.) Setting Up a Space for Your Labradoodle

Before you bring your Labradoodle puppy home, I would recommend setting up a particular area of your house that your dog can call his own. Labradoodle puppies are cute and cuddly, but they also have a tendency to get into trouble so you need to have some kind of area set up where your puppy can play without you having to worry about what he is getting into. What I did for my Labradoodle was purchase a puppy playpen. I set it up in the den in my house – a room that isn't exactly secluded but generally isn't crowded either. I placed my puppy's crate in the playpen along with his food and water bowls and his favorite toys. When I was done, it was like my puppy had a little room of his own!

If you don't have a lot of extra space in your home to do something like this, you might be able just to use a baby gate to close off a small room like the laundry room or a half bathroom. The key is to keep your puppy from wandering around the house unsupervised without having to confine him to the crate. Let me say right now that there is nothing wrong with crating a puppy, however, as long as you do it correctly. I'll get into the details of how to use a crate correctly during the training section of this book – you'll find that information in Chapter Six.

To make things easier on yourself I would personally recommend choosing a location that doesn't have carpeting. Sure, wood flooring can be damaged by liquid, but you probably don't have to worry about it if you clean up any accidents fairly quickly. If your only option is a carpeted room, you can try putting down an old blanket as an extra layer of protection or use some plastic sheeting. During crate training, you'll be letting your puppy out every hour or two, so the risk for him having an accident will be relatively low, but there is no harm in making things easy for yourself just in case of an accident.

Once you've decided where you want to set up your puppy's area, you then need to outfit it properly. Place your puppy's crate inside the playpen and line it with a comfy bed or blanket. You may want to use an old blanket for a little while until your Labradoodle puppy is housetrained – you don't want to have to throw out an expensive dog bed if he has an accident! You should also keep a basket of your puppy's toys nearby as well as his food and water bowls. Don't put food or water bowls in your puppy's crate, however, because it could interfere with your crate training efforts. Just keep them nearby, so your puppy doesn't have to go far when he needs a snack or a drink of water.

b.) Labradoodle Energy and Exercise Needs

If you want to know exactly what to expect from your Labradoodle in terms of his energy level and exercise needs, you will be disappointed. As I have mentioned several times over by now, designer dog breeds are a little unpredictable when it comes to specific traits. In order to predict the activity level of the Labradoodle, you have to consider the energy levels of both the Poodle and the Labrador Retriever.

As you may already know, the Labrador Retriever is one of the most energetic dog breeds out there. These dogs are always running on a full tank, and they never turn down an opportunity to play. Poodles are a little more reserved, though they are still a relatively active breed. The Toy and Miniature versions of the Poodle breed may not be quite as high-energy as the Standard Poodle, but all three versions need a good bit of daily exercise. When it comes to the Labradoodle, you should expect your dog to have a relatively high level of energy and high needs for exercise as well.

To make sure that your Labradoodle gets the exercise he needs to burn off his energy you should plan on taking him for at least one 30-minute walk daily. If you can only manage 30 minutes of exercise for your Labradoodle, you should try to work in some active playtime as well – find your dog some interactive toys and let him loose in the backyard to work off his energy by himself or with another dog. You will quickly learn from experience that a Labradoodle, who doesn't get enough exercise quickly, becomes mischievous and often destructive.

Another important thing I want you to understand about the Labradoodle breed is that these dogs require a lot of mental exercise – not just physical exercise. Labradoodles are a very intelligent breed, so their brains need to be stimulated and exercised just as much as their bodies do. To meet your dog's needs for mental stimulation, you can give him some interactive toys or puzzle toys, and you can engage him in training games. Training your Labradoodle to perform a job or to participate in dog sports is an excellent way to provide both mental and physical stimulation so consider that option as well!

c.) Recommended Labradoodle Accessories

I've already given you an overview of the Labradoodle's requirements for space and exercise, but you might be thinking that it would be good to have a list of all the accessories you will need. Well, here it is! <u>Below you will find a list of the top accessories and equipment I think you will find useful as a Labradoodle owner</u>:

- **Sturdy dog crate** – You will be using the crate a lot when it comes time for housetraining but, until then, your puppy can use the crate to sleep in.

- **Dog bed or blanket** – To make the crate more comfortable for your puppy, line it with a dog bed or blanket – you might want to start with something you don't mind throwing away, just in case.

- **Food and water bowls** – The best materials for food and water bowls are stainless steel or ceramic. These options are easy to clean, and they don't harbor bacteria.

- **An assortment of toys** – Your Labradoodle puppy will need plenty of toys to keep him busy so don't skimp on the selection! Once you learn which toys your puppy likes best you can stick to those and replace them as needed.

- **Grooming supplies** – Depending on the type and length of coat your Labradoodle has you may need a wire pin brush, a wide-toothed comb, and a slicker brush. You should also have some dog shampoo on hand as well as doggie ear cleaning solution, dog toothpaste, and a dog-friendly toothbrush.

- **Collar and leash** – If you plan on taking your Labradoodle out of the house you will need a collar and leash. Make sure your dog's collar carries his ID tag and choose a collar and leash proportionate to his size. This means you'll probably have to buy several sizes throughout your dog's life.

- **Harness** – I personally recommend using a harness when you walk your Labradoodle instead of just the collar. If you have to tug on the leash to correct or guide your dog it can put dangerous pressure on his neck – a harness will distribute the force across his back which is much safer.

There are plenty of other accessories which might come in handy for you as a dog owner, but these are the basic things I think all dog owners should have on hand. As you gain experience caring for your Labradoodle you may discover some other things you find useful – you can also talk to other experienced dog owners for suggestions.

2.) *Labradoodle Dog Nutrition*

If you want your Labradoodle to remain happy and healthy, the best thing you can do for him is to choose a high-quality diet.

If someone were to ask you what the best thing you can do to ensure your Labradoodle's long-term health and wellness was, how would you answer them? Before I became a dog owner myself, I probably would have said something about vaccinations or regular vet check-ups – the thought of dog food wouldn't have even entered my mind. What I have learned (from personal experience, unfortunately) however, is that buying your dog a high-quality dog food is absolutely the best thing you can do to make sure that he stays healthy. Let me tell you how I know this to be true.

After I had picked out my first Labradoodle puppy, Sandy, from the breeder, I stopped at the pet store on my way home to stock up on supplies. When I got to the pet store, I headed straight for the dog food section and quickly realized that there were more options than I had anticipated. I spent a few minutes poking around then I grabbed something with a picture of a happy dog on it and headed for the checkout.

When I finally got to bring my Sandy home, I started feeding him the food I had purchased. He grew like a weed for the first couple of weeks and by the time he was six months old he was probably ten times the size he was when I'd gotten him. I could be exaggerating a little bit, but the important thing is that he had grown – fast. As Sandy grew to adulthood, I made sure he had all of his vaccinations and always took him to the vet on time. But I started to notice some problems. Sandy wasn't as active and energetic as I had heard Labradoodles should be and he was starting to have digestive problems as well.

When I took him to the vet, the first question he asked was, "what are you feeding him?" I am a little embarrassed to admit that I only knew the brand name of the dog food I had chosen – I couldn't have told you what was in it at the time. What the vet said to me, however, had me rushing home to read the label on the package. What I found was a whole bunch of ingredients that I didn't even know existed – things like corn gluten meal and poultry by-product meal. It soon became very clear to me that what I was feeding Sandy was little better than garbage.

At that point, I knew that I had to make a change or Sandy was going to keep suffering for my mistakes. So, I buckled down and did the research to learn more about my dog's nutritional needs – I also learned how to read a pet food label so I would know a quality product when I saw it. It took a few days of hard research but eventually I felt confident enough to head back to the pet store.

I arrived with several brand names in mind and walked up and down the aisles until I found them. I was a little shocked by the price tag, but I knew that my Sandy's health was worth it. I brought home the new food, transitioned him onto it over the next week or so, and waited to see what would happen. Well, let me tell you – the transformation was amazing! Sandy blossomed into this energetic, youthful dog with a soft, shining coat, bright eyes, and boundless enthusiasm for life. I finally had the dog I had always wanted, and I vowed never to take my dog's health for granted again. To this day I still research everything I put into my dog's body to make sure that it won't harm him in any way, and I encourage you to take this same proactive approach to your Labradoodle's health and nutrition!

Now, I don't expect you to do exactly what I did – to spend four days on the Internet researching different dog foods. I do, however, encourage you to take to heart the information I am about to give you. I will tell you what you need to know in terms of the basic nutritional needs of Labradoodle dogs and give you some key tips for choosing a quality dog food. I will also give you some helpful tips for feeding Labradoodles in general as well as a list of dangerous foods to avoid. Your dog's health and wellness is a gift that should be treasured so do not take it for granted like I once did!

a.) Nutritional Needs for Labradoodle Dogs

As you probably already know, dogs are carnivorous animals – but what does that really mean? It means that the dog's body is designed to derive the majority of its nutrition from animal products, not plant products. All living things need a balance of protein, fats, and carbohydrate in their diet as well as fresh water, vitamins, and minerals. For dogs, however, protein is the most important nutritional consideration – it provides your dog with the building blocks for healthy muscles and tissues. Fat is the second most important because it provides a highly concentrated source of energy. Carbohydrates provide dietary fiber as well as key nutrients, but your dog has a very limited ability to digest plant materials, so the type of carbohydrates in his food need to be carefully selected.

In terms of protein, puppies need to have at least 22% of their diet from protein sources and adult dogs need at least 18%. It is always better, however, to have higher protein content than the minimum. Proteins are made up of amino acids – there are 22 of them, but your Labradoodle's body is only able to synthesize (or create) 12 of them. The rest are called essential amino acids, and they must come from your dog's food. A complete protein source (like meat, poultry, fish, or eggs) is one that contains all ten essential amino acids, so these are the protein sources that are the most nutritionally valuable for your dog.

When it comes to fats, puppies need a minimum of 8% fat and adult dogs need a minimum of 5%. For Labradoodles, fats should come from animal-based sources as well. Essential fatty acids are important for your dog's skin and coat health, plus they play a role in immune health as well. Even though fat might sound like an unhealthy ingredient to you, it is crucial for your dog. Chicken fat, for example, might sound gross to you but it is a valuable ingredient in dog food – fish oils like salmon oil, or menhaden oil are also valuable additions.

A dog's body is designed to derive the majority of its nutrition from protein and fat, but it is still capable of processing a limited amount of carbohydrate. Carbohydrates provide your dog with dietary fiber to support healthy digestion, and they also provide some essential vitamins and minerals. Dogs have a limited ability to digest high-fiber foods, however, so the carbohydrates in your dog's diet need to come from digestible sources - primarily cooked whole grains like brown rice and oatmeal as well as gluten-free alternatives like potatoes, peas, and sweet potatoes.

As I've already mentioned, the higher the protein content of your dog's food, the better. The fat content should be moderate – too much fat can lead to excess weight gain in dogs, and too little can be bad for his health. When it comes to carbohydrates, however, dogs do not have any specific requirements in terms of percentages. More important than the amount of carbohydrate is the type – it should be highly digestible and as minimally processed as possible.

b.) Choosing a Healthy Dog Food

Now that you have a better understanding of your Labradoodle's nutritional needs you may be curious to learn about what a high-quality dog food looks like. The most important thing you need to know about dog food is that, in most cases, the cheaper the food, the lower the quality. Many low-quality pet food manufacturers use non-nutritive fillers to bulk up their products while keeping costs low. Remember the corn gluten meal I mentioned earlier? That's what I'm talking about – corn, wheat, and soy ingredients are generally low in nutritional value for dogs, and they have no place in a quality diet.

Before I get into the details about what goes into a good dog food, I'll give you a little peak into how much you should be prepared to spend. A large bag of low-quality dog food might cost about $15 while a large bag of a high-quality, all-natural dog food could cost as much as $50 (€44.50). Before you get too worried, remember that there are options in between these two spectrums. You can still find a quality dog food made with real ingredients in the $30 (€26.70) range and feel good that your dog is getting the nutrients he needs. If you feed him a low-quality diet, you may end up spending more in the long run for vet bills because he may develop nutritional deficiencies or other health problems.

Now let's get into the details about how to identify a high-quality dog food. In general, there are three things you should look for on the dog food label – the AAFCO statement of nutritional adequacy, the guaranteed analysis, and the ingredients list. The American Association of Feed Control Officials (AAFCO) has established profiles for the minimum nutritional requirements for dogs in different life stages. They evaluate commercial pet food products, comparing them to those profiles, to determine if they are complete and balanced for the intended animal. If the product meets those requirements the package will have some sort of statement on it that looks something like this:

"[Product] is formulated to meet the nutritional levels established by the AAFCO Dog Food nutrient profiles for [Life Stage]."

If the dog food product you are looking at carries this statement you can rest assured that it will at least meet the basic nutritional needs for your Labradoodle. It is important to realize, however, that nutritional adequacy does not necessarily imply quality. A low-quality dog food could still meet your dog's basic nutritional needs. That is why you need to look at other parts of the pet food package as well – the next place to look is the guaranteed analysis. This is the part of the label that tells you how much crude protein, crude fat, and crude fiber the product contains – it also tells you how much moisture is in it. This is an excellent tool to use in comparing different dog food products.

In addition to making sure that the dog food you're looking at meets the minimum requirements, I mentioned in the last section that you should make sure that there are plenty of high-quality ingredients on the ingredients list, starting with protein, of course. The ingredients list on a dog food package is organized in descending order by volume – the ingredients at the top of the list are used in the highest quantity measured by volume.

When you read the ingredients list, you want to see high-quality ingredients throughout, but you want to see a quality protein source at the very top. Fresh meats like chicken, turkey, lamb, and fish are good protein sources for dogs like the Labradoodle. Do not freak out if you see the word "meal" attached to a meat ingredient, either. Meat meals are already cooked to a moisture level around 10%, so they are a much more concentrated source of protein than fresh meats which contain as much as 80% moisture. In addition to quality proteins, you also want to see animal fats and digestible carbohydrates on the list. It is okay if the product has more than one carbohydrate as long as they are both quality sources, but be wary of any product that has more than two or three carbohydrates – especially if they come from corn, wheat, or soy ingredients which have limited nutritional value for dogs.

Some other beneficial additives for high-quality dog foods include prebiotics, probiotics, and chelated minerals. Many quality dog foods use dried fermentation products in their recipes – these act as probiotics, helping to support your Labradoodle's digestive system. Chelated minerals are simply minerals that have been chemically bonded to protein molecules – this makes them easier for your dog's body to digest and absorb. Vitamin supplements can also be beneficial, but it is always better to see natural sources of vitamins and minerals like fresh fruits and vegetables instead of synthetic supplements.

When evaluating the quality of a pet food product not only should you pay attention to the ingredients that ARE included in the list, but you should also make note of the things that AREN'T there. Avoid products made with artificial additives like colors, flavors, and preservatives. You should also avoid products made with by-products and low-quality fillers. If the list is full of unidentifiable ingredients or things that sound like chemicals, it probably isn't a quality product. You want to see plenty of fresh meats, animal fats, digestible carbohydrates, and fruits and vegetables on the list.

c.) Tips for Feeding Labradoodles

While all dogs have the same basic nutritional requirements, the specific needs of different breeds are sometimes unique. For example, small-breed dogs need more calories per pound of bodyweight than large-breed dogs because their metabolisms are very fast. That is why small-breed dog foods are usually higher in fat content than the average kibble. Large-breed dogs may need more calories in general but, if you do the math, you'll find that the number of calories per pound of bodyweight is lower for large-breed dogs.

Determining the calorie needs of your Labradoodle can be tricky because there are different sizes for this breed. The Standard Labradoodle can range in size from 50 to 65 pounds (22.7 to 29.5 kg) which can be considered a large breed. The Miniature Labradoodle, however, is a small to medium breed, and the Medium Labradoodle is a medium breed. When it comes to commercial dog foods, most brands that offer size-specific formulas do not offer a medium-breed formula. If you have a Standard Labradoodle, pick a regular adult formula or a large-breed adult formula and, for Miniature Labradoodles, consider a small-breed formula.

When it comes to determining how much to feed your Labradoodle, your best bet is to follow the feeding recommendations on the pet food package. Feed your dog the recommended amount for a few weeks and keep an eye on his weight and condition. If your Labradoodle dog gains too much weight you can reduce his daily portion – if he loses weight or appears to be lacking energy, increase his portion. You can also consult your veterinarian if you need help determining how much to feed your dog.

Not only do you need to know how much to feed your Labradoodle but you also have to decide how often to feed him. Smaller Labradoodles can benefit from three meals a day while larger ones can get away with two. I generally recommend at least 2 meals a day for all dogs, though mine actually gets three because I am home during the day. However many meals you decide on, just be sure the total amount your dog gets lines up with the feeding recommendations. You can also give your dog treats (especially during training), but they shouldn't make up more than 10% of his daily diet.

d.) Dangerous Foods to Avoid for Dogs

When you bring your Labradoodle home, and the two of you start getting to know each other you will come to realize something about your dog – he loves food. Your dog doesn't care what kind of food it is or where it comes from; he just wants to eat it. It is your job as the dog owner to understand which foods are healthy for your dog and which ones aren't. <u>Below you will find a list of food ingredients that can be harmful or even deadly for dogs</u>:

- Alcohol/beer
- Apple seeds
- Avocado
- Cherry pits
- Chocolate
- Coffee
- Garlic
- Grapes/raisins
- Macadamia nuts
- Mold
- Mushrooms
- Mustard seeds
- Onions/leeks
- Peach pits
- Potato leaves/stems
- Rhubarb leaves
- Tea
- Tomato leaves/stems
- Walnuts
- Xylitol
- Yeast dough

If your Labradoodle dog eats any of these foods, you need to contact the Pet Poison Control hotline right away at (888) 426 – 4435. They will help you determine what the best course of action is to take.

3.) *Labradoodle Grooming Information*

Labradoodles inherit their curly coats from the Poodle which means they have a lot of hair! Be prepared to groom your dog frequently to control shedding.

The Labradoodle has a beautiful curly or wavy coat that comes in a variety of different colors. Making sure that your dog gets a healthy diet will help to preserve the condition of his skin and coat, but regular grooming is required as well. The tricky part about grooming Labradoodles is the fact that each dog's coat will be a little bit different depending on breeding. It might take some experimentation to determine which brush and which grooming style works best for your dog but once you figure it out you can make it a routine.

a.) Brushing and Bathing Your Labradoodle

Although the Poodle as a very low-shedding coat, the Labrador Retriever's coat is thick and it sheds quite a bit. The Labradoodle can be a show-shedding breed, though that is not always the case. Even if your Labradoodle doesn't shed a whole lot, you should still brush his coat a few times a week at the minimum. Brushing your dog's coat helps to distribute the natural oils produced in his skin – these oils help to keep his coat shiny and soft, plus they also create a layer of protection.

When brushing your Labradoodle's coat, you should start by checking him for mats and tangles. If you find any, try to work through them gently with your fingers or with a wide-toothed comb – only cut the mat out if it is absolutely necessary. Once you've checked for mats, start brushing your dog's coat at the back of the head, working your way down the neck and along the back. Always brush in the direction of hair growth and do not pull too hard on the brush if it gets caught. Once your Labradoodle's back has been brushed out, work your way down his legs one at a time and don't forget the chest and abdomen.

Each Labradoodle's coat is a little different, but you can expect the hair to grow fairly long. If you plan to show your Labradoodle you might choose to keep his coat natural and just style it for the show. If you want to minimize shedding and maintenance, however, you might be better of clipping it short. A puppy clip is a popular cut for the Labradoodle – it just involves shortening the hair uniformly all over the body. Another option is the pet clip which follows the contours of the dog's body but is still a little shorter than the show clip.

It is generally a good idea to have your Labradoodle groomed by a professional groomer, though you can certainly brush him at home and you can also bathe him at home as needed. To bathe your dog, make sure that you brush him first to get rid of any dead hairs. Then, fill the tub with a few inches of lukewarm water and have your Labradoodle get in. Use a cup or a hand sprayer to wet down your dog's coat then use a little bit of dog-friendly shampoo and work it into a thick lather. Rinse the coat well until you've gotten rid of all of the shampoo and then towel your dog dry.

b.) Cleaning Your Labradoodle's Ears

The Labradoodle has flop ears which means that they hang down on either side of the dog's head. Dog breeds with floppy ears covered in hair tend to experience frequent ear infections because the inner ear doesn't get enough air circulation. If your Labradoodle's ears get wet, they become a breeding ground for bacteria, and that can lead to infection.

I personally recommend cleaning your Labradoodle's ears once a week just to be safe. To clean your dog's ears, squeeze a few drops of dog ear cleaner into the ear canal then massage the base of your dog's ear to distribute the solution. Use a clean cotton ball or swab to remove wax and debris as well as any excess solution then let your dog's ears air-dry. It only takes a few minutes, but it can help to prevent infections!

c.) Brushing Your Labradoodle's Teeth

The thought of brushing your dog's teeth might sound strange to you, but dental hygiene is just as important for dogs as it is for humans. You may be surprised to learn that a large percentage of dogs exhibit signs of dental disease by the time they reach three years old. Brushing your Labradoodle's teeth on a regular basis only takes a few minutes, but it can go a long way toward preventing dental disease and other dental problems.

The key to brushing your Labradoodle's teeth is to start early. When your dog is still young you should get him used to having his mouth and teeth touched – be gentle but work with him often so he gets used to this type of handling. You can use a special dog toothbrush or a rubber fitting that goes over your finger. Use a small amount of dog toothpaste and clean a few of your dog's teeth each time you do it. Some Labradoodles will let you brush all of their teeth at once, though some have a very limited tolerance so you might need to brush just a few at a time, aiming to brush all of his teeth over the course of the week.

d.) Clipping Your Dog's Nails

One of the grooming tasks that many dog owners overlook is clipping the dog's nails. Many people assume that a dog's nails are supposed to be long or that they will be naturally filed down. Unless your Labradoodle spends a lot of time outside, however, his nails can easily become overgrown. You should plan to trim your dog's nails once every week or two. The more frequently you trim the dog's nails, the less you will have to take off which reduces the risk that you might cut the nail too short.

Before you trim your Labradoodle's nails for the first time, it is a good idea to have your vet or groomer show you how. A dog's nail contains a blood vessel called the quick which provides the blood supply to the nail. If you cut your dog's nail too short you could sever the quick – this will not only be painful for your dog, but it will likely cause profuse bleeding as well. Your best bet is to trim the minimum amount of nail each time and to do it frequently enough that the nails don't become overgrown.

Chapter Six: Labradoodle Training Guide

The Labradoodle is a friendly and fun-loving breed, and they are also intelligent – this means they respond well to training.

Though many people love the Labradoodle breed for its beautiful curly coat and friendly temperament, their level of intelligence is a huge benefit as well. The smarter the dog, the more quickly it responds to training – this makes your life as a dog owner infinitely easier. Labradoodles are highly intelligent, and it isn't uncommon for them to learn a new command with just three or four repetitions. It is important, however, that you use the right training method. In this chapter, I'll give you an overview of different training methods and give you some specific tips for training and housebreaking your Labradoodle.

1.) Overview of Popular Training Methods

If you talk to five different dog trainers, you will receive five different recommendations in terms of the best training method to use for Labradoodles. Every dog trainer has his own way of doing things but, for the most part, dog training methods can be divided into a few categories. Before I go into the details, I want to stress the importance of building and maintaining a positive relationship with your dog. To you, your dog might simply be a friend and a companion but, to your dog, you are his everything. The way you treat him during training and on a day-to-day basis will have a significant impact on the kind of relationship you have – don't do anything that might damage it!

While there are plenty of variations out there, most dog training methods can be broken into three categories: dominance training, scientific training, and positive reinforcement training. In the following pages, I'm going to give you an overview of each so you can make your own choice, but I will also tell you about which method I used for my own Labradoodles.

Dominance Training – If you have ever watched an episode of The Dog Whisperer show with Cesar Milan, you have seen an example of dominance training. This type of training hinges on the idea that dogs are pack animals, and it is your job as the dog's owner to become the alpha. Trainers that use this method of dog training suggest that dogs exhibit bad behaviors because they are trying to assert their dominance over the owner – correction must be used to decrease these behaviors and to establish the owner as the dominant force in the household.

This type of training can be useful for certain situations such as teaching a dog not to perform a specific behavior – like pulling on the leash during a walk or using a shock collar to discourage barking. Unfortunately, this training method also has the potential to create an attitude of fear in your household. The more you punish your dog, the more he will come to fear you. In many cases, dogs do not understand it when their owners punish them unless the punishment immediately follows the crime. This is why rubbing your dog's nose in the mess is ineffective as a way of teaching him not to have an accident in the house – your dog won't understand what you're doing, and he certainly won't learn from the punishment.

Another problem with this type of training is that it really only works in single-owner households – your whole family cannot be the alpha. If you treat your dog one way, and someone else in your family treats him another way, it is likely that your dog will become confused, and that can cause stress for both of you. In the end, most dog trainers agree that punishment-based training methods are not the most efficient option for dogs.

Scientific Training – This type of training incorporates some of the principles of dominance training in the fact that you end up using consequences (both positive and negative) to influence your dog's behavior. To utilize this method of training, you reward your dog for desired behaviors in order to increase the chances that he will repeat that behavior. Plus, you remove the reward to discourage undesired behaviors. This type of training is inspired by the behavioral research performed by B.F. Skinner, an American psychologist.

To utilize this method of training, you would first teach your dog to perform desired behaviors by using a reward system to reinforce them. At the same time, you must also teach your dog that undesired behaviors don't work. For example, if you are playing with your dog and want to teach him not to jump at the toy in your hand, you simply remove the toy when he performs the undesired behavior to teach him that that sort of behavior doesn't get him what he wants. In this way, you discourage the undesired behavior without using punishment.

Positive Reinforcement Training – This is the most popular training method and, according to many trainers, the most effective method as well. Positive reinforcement training utilizes the rewards-based principles of scientific training to encourage dogs to repeat desired behaviors and to help the dog learn to associate those behaviors with specific commands. For example, if you want your dog to learn how to sit when you give him the Sit command, you simply reward him for doing so. With a few repetitions, your dog will learn to associate the action with the command and the reward will encourage him to repeat it each time you use the command.

Many dog training methods incorporate bits and pieces from each of these training types. In the end, it is your choice which option you choose, and you may find that your training style doesn't fit neatly into any one category.

2.) *The Best Labradoodle Training Style*

The training style you choose for your Labradoodle will have a significant impact on how quickly your dog responds and how well he learns.

Now that you have a deeper understanding of how different dog training methods work, you may be curious to know which Labradoodle training style I prefer. One thing I want to stress before I tell you about what I DO use with my dog is to tell you what I do NOT do. I absolutely never punish my Labradoodles by hitting them or yelling at them. The Labradoodle is a very gentle breed, and they are smart enough to follow your cues and to learn everything you have to teach them – there simply is no need for punishment if you go about your training correctly.

The Labradoodle training method I prefer is positive reinforcement training with a rewards-based system. If I want my Labradoodle to do something, I simply encourage him to do it and then reward him when he does. All dogs love treats, so giving your dog a treat for doing what you want him to do is a straightforward and effective way to ensure that he repeats that behavior in the future. This type of training can be used to teach your dog everything from a simple Sit and Stay command to more complex tricks.

To give you a better idea what I mean, here is an example of the training sequence I used when I was teaching Sandy to respond to the Sit command:

1. Kneel down in front of your Labradoodle dog and hold a small treat between the thumb and forefinger of your dominant hand.

2. Get your dog's attention with the treat by waving it in front of his nose so he catches the smell.

3. Hold the treat just in front of your dog's nose and tell him to "Sit" in a firm and clear tone.

4. Immediately move the treat up and forward toward the back of your dog's head.

5. Your Labradoodle should lift his nose to follow the treat and, in doing so, his bottom will lower to the floor – if he doesn't respond this way, start over.

6. As soon as your dog's bottom hits the floor, tell him "Good dog" and give him the treat.

7. Repeat this training sequence several times until your Labradoodle responds consistently with the appropriate behavior.

8. Continue practicing with your dog, slowly reducing the frequency of food rewards but remaining consistent with verbal praise.

Do you see now how this type of training works? The key to positive reinforcement training is to be consistent – consistent in using the same command each time and in praising or rewarding your dog for following it. Like I said earlier, Labradoodles are very smart, so it will only take a few repetitions for your dog to learn what the command means. At this point you can reduce the food rewards, offering them every other time or only once in a while. You should always praise your dog for responding properly, however, to keep him motivated to follow your commands in the future. Instead of food rewards you can also use what I call "life" rewards: a belly rub or a few seconds of playtime with a favorite toy. If your dog likes something, use it as a reward!

3.) Labradoodle Crate Training Guide

Having a deeper understanding of the positive reinforcement method for Labradoodle training will help you to understand how my preferred method of housebreaking works for dogs. I personally ascribe to the crate training method. Before you write me off, thinking that keeping a dog in a crate is cruel, I want to tell you something. My Labradoodles love their crates. Whenever Layla is tired and wants to take a nap, where does she go? Her crate! I don't have to tell her to go there; she just knows that it is a safe, comfortable place where she can rest and relax if she needs to.

At this point, you might still be a little skeptical, or you might think that my dog is strange. What I want you to realize, however, is that the only time when putting a dog in a crate is cruel is if it is a method of punishment – it would also be cruel if you kept the dog in the crate for an extended period of time without a break. If you teach your dog to regard the crate as his own personal little space, however, he will come to like it. That is the key to success with crate training.

Before you actually start crate training your Labradoodle puppy you should take some time to get him used to the crate and to start forming a positive association. You can do this by feeding him his meals in the crate with the door open, and you can involve the crate in play time by tossing treats into it for your puppy to find. Once he is comfortable going into and out of the crate you can start closing the door behind him for a few seconds at a time then work your way up to an hour or more.

Once your puppy is able to remain calm and comfortable in the crate for a few hours at a time, he is ready for crate training. Here is my step-by-step guide for crate training your Labradoodle puppy:

1. Choose a specific part of your backyard where you want your Labradoodle puppy to do his business – you can fence off a small area or simply choose a particular corner.

2. Take your puppy outside every hour or two and lead him directly to this chosen location each and every time you take him out.

3. Tell your Labradoodle "Go pee" (or choose another simple command) as soon as he gets to that particular area.

4. Wait for your Labradoodle puppy to do his business – if he does, immediately praise him in a very excited voice and give him a small treat as a reward.

5. If your Labradoodle doesn't have to go, immediately take him back inside instead of letting him wander.

6. Keep a close eye on your Labradoodle at all times when he is in the house – try to confine him to whatever room you are in so you can watch him.

7. Watch your Labradoodle for signs that he has to go and take him outside immediately if he starts to sniff the ground, walk in circles, or squat – this is in addition to taking him out every hour or two.

8. When you cannot physically watch your Labradoodle, keep him confined to his crate to reduce the risk of him having an accident – do not keep any food or water in the crate with him.

9. Limit your dog's time in the crate to just a few hours until he is old enough to hold his bladder and bowels for a longer period of time.

10. Always let your Labradoodle dog outside immediately before putting him in the crate and after

releasing him – you should also take him out after a meal or after a nap.

Remember, the key to success with dog training is consistency! If you are firm about making sure your Labradoodle only does his business outside, and you are consistent about rewarding him for doing so, he will learn quickly. My Sandy was almost completely housebroken in just under 3 weeks!

Chapter Seven: Labradoodle Breeding and Labradoodle Puppies

Labradoodle puppies are the most adorable thing ever, but they require a lot of care so don't take the idea of breeding lightly!

Because the Labradoodle is such an amazing breed, it can be tempting to breed your dog just so you have a chance to enjoy a little of Labradoodle puppies. What you may not realize, however, is that there is a lot of time and effort that goes into breeding dogs and raising a litter of puppies. I highly recommend doing your research before you decide to breed your Labradoodle. In this chapter, I will give you a general idea of what to expect when breeding dogs as well as some detailed information about raising Labradoodle puppies. This information is provided for your reference only – if you actually choose to breed your dog, you will need to do a lot more research on your own.

1.) General Labradoodle Breeding Information

When you first start to consider breeding your Labradoodle it might sound like a very good idea. After all, what is better than a litter of Labradoodle puppies? What you have to realize, however, is that breeding dogs are expensive, and it can also be dangerous – there are a lot of complications that could occur during the pregnancy or during birth. You should absolutely not breed your dog is your primary motivation is to make money. The only reason you should breed your dog is if you want to improve or preserve the breed.

a.) What is an F1b Labradoodle? Hybrid Genetics

The Labradoodle is a designer dog – it is a cross between two pure breeds. When you breed a purebred dog to a purebred dog (a purebred is 100% genetically pure) you get a hybrid – the first generation of such a crossing is labeled F1. If you breed two F1 hybrids together, you get a litter of hybrid puppies which are labeled F2, or second generation. Crossing two F2 hybrids together will also result in a litter of hybrid puppies which will be labeled F3, or third generation. These are the most basic crossings that can be done to create a hybrid like the Labradoodle, but they are not the only options.

In addition to these standard crossings, there is also a common breeding practice called backcrossing – this is when you breed a first generation (F1) hybrid back to a purebred dog. In the case of the Labradoodle, this would involve breeding an F1 Labradoodle with either a purebred Poodle or a purebred Labrador Retriever. The resulting litter would exhibit a higher degree of similarity to the purebred parent and would be labeled F1b. You can also breed an F1 hybrid to an F1b backcross dog to create a second-generation backcrossed dog (F2b).

b.) Basic Dog Breeding Information

While the exact details vary a little bit from one breed to another, the basics of dog breeding are largely the same in most cases. When a female dog is mature enough for breeding, she will start to go through the estrus cycle, also known as "heat." Most dog breeds experience their first heat around 6 months of age – this is why you should spay your female Labradoodle before this age if you do not plan to breed her. It is important to note that while your dog's body may be physically capable of breeding at this age, it is not recommended that you breed her during her first heat cycle – wait until she is 18 months old.

The heat cycle for female dogs occurs twice a year in most cases, though some small-breed dogs will go into heat three times per year. The Labradoodle can be either a small-, medium-, or large-breed dog so you will have to keep an eye on your dog's individual cycle. The heat cycle lasts between 2 and 4 weeks with an average length of about 21 days or most dogs. During the heat cycle, your dog's ovaries will release eggs and, if she is mated to an intact male dog during this period, conception will occur, and the dog will become pregnant.

<u>Some of the signs that indicate your female Labradoodle dog is going into heat may include</u>:

- Swelling of the external vulva
- Bloody discharge from the vaginal area
- Increased frequency of urination, urine marking
- Vocalization, whining or howling

The swelling of the vulva is usually the first sign of heat in most dogs, though some develop a discharge first. The color and thickness of that discharge will change throughout the course of the heat cycle, and you can use it to tell what stage of the cycle your dog is in. At first, the discharge is usually fairly red and bloody, but it will become waterier and pink in color about 7 to 10 days into the cycle – this is the point at which your dog is most fertile so you should introduce her to the male dog at this point. Keep in mind, however, that sperm can survive in the female's reproductive tract for 5 to 7 days, so pregnancy can occur even days after mating.

If your female Labradoodle dog becomes pregnant, then she will go into something called the gestation period; this is the period of time during which the eggs developed into fetuses inside her uterus. The gestation period for most dogs lasts between 61 and 65 days, about 9 weeks, but the average length is 63 days. At the end of the gestation period, the dog will whelp the puppies (give birth), and she will care for them until they are old enough to become independent.

c.) Breeding Risks and Precautions

Before you actual decide to breed your Labradoodle, you need to understand the potential risks involved and take the necessary steps to mitigate them. Breeding puts a lot of strain on a female dog's body – if you breed your Labradoodle too early she could be too young to carry a litter to term or she could experience dangerous complications during the birth. The risks for male dogs that are associated with breeding are much lower, though there are still some potential problems that come with leaving a male dog intact instead of having him neutered.

As a general rule, male dogs should not be used in breeding prior to 1 year of age, and they should not be used after 12 years of age. Females should not be bred prior to 18 months of age or after 8 years. Both males and females need to be in good health, free of any communicable disease, and free from genetic faults. They should also be examined by a veterinarian to rule out hereditary eye diseases. In addition to following these general rules, you should also have your female Labradoodle dog thoroughly checked out by a veterinarian before breeding to ensure that she is healthy enough and mature enough to bear a litter.

2.) *Raising Labradoodle Puppies*

What could be cuter than a litter of newborn Labradoodle
puppies? As cute as they are, raising puppies is a big
responsibility, and it can be expensive too!

While your dog is pregnant, you will want to keep a
close eye on her to make sure that she doesn't experience
any complications from the pregnancy. Most vets
recommend feeding your pregnant dog the same amount of
food until she reaches the late stages of pregnancy. If you
don't really know how much you should be feeding your
dog, just let her feed freely – she will know how much she
needs, and she will stop when she is full. You should still

check with your veterinarian, however, to make sure that she is gaining weight at a healthy rate.

During the late stages of pregnancy, you will need to start preparing for delivery. The only way you will know when your dog is approaching her due date is if you keep track of her cycle and record the day on which she was mated. Remember, the gestation period for dogs lasts anywhere from 61 to 65 days, so mark your calendar with the expected due date. Near the end of the gestation period, you will need to provide your Labradoodle with a safe place to whelp her puppies. A nice big box in a dark, quiet area is a good option. Just line it with newspaper and old towels that you don't mind getting dirty – you can throw them out and replace them after the birth.

When your dog starts to get closer to her due date, she will probably spend more and more time in the whelping box. Not only is she preparing to give birth, but it can be challenging and uncomfortable for her to move much once the puppies get bigger inside her. Try not to disturb your dog, but keep an eye on her within a few days of the due date and watch for the signs of labor. The best way to predict when the puppies will be born is to start taking her internal temperature within a few days of her due date. The average internal temperature for a dog is between 100°F to 102°F (37.7°C to 38.8°C). Once it drops to about 98°F (36.6°C), labor is likely to begin within the hour.

Aside from the change in body temperature, you will be able to tell that labor is starting when your Labradoodle begins to show obvious signs of discomfort like pacing, panting, and changing positions. When your dog starts to give birth, stay nearby but let her do it on her own. In the early stages of labor, contractors will occur about 10 minutes apart. If your Labradoodle has contractions for more than 2 hours without giving birth, take her to the emergency vet immediately. When she does start giving birth, she will whelp one puppy about every half hour.

After each Labradoodle puppy is born, the mother dog will tear open the birth sac and bite through the umbilical cord. She will then clean the puppy and lick him to stimulate his breathing before the next puppy is born. After all of the puppies have been born, your mother dog will expel the afterbirth. You shouldn't be surprised if she eats it – it is rich in nutrients, and she needs some extra energy at this point. Make sure that your newborn Labradoodle puppies begin nursing within an hour of being born, so they get some of the colostrum. Colostrum is simply the name of the first milk the mother produces and it is full of nutrients and antibodies from the mother's immune system. The puppies will rely on these antibodies for protection until their own immune systems develop.

The litter size for Labradoodles can be as small as 4 or as large as 15, though the average number of puppies is 8. When they are born, Labradoodle puppies are very small; they are also blind, deaf, and nearly hairless. The puppies will be completely dependent on the mother for heat and food for at least a few weeks. The puppies will begin to crawl between 7 and 14 days, and they should be able to walk by 21 days. The teeth begin to erupt between 2 and 4 weeks of age, and all of the teeth should have grown in by the time the puppies are 8 weeks old. Their ears will open around day 14, and they may start eating small amounts of softened solid food around 3 weeks of age.

By the time the Labradoodle puppies are 5 weeks old, they will be playing with each other, and their personalities will start to develop. Over the next two to three weeks the puppies should be given more soft food to encourage them to wean off their mother's milk. At 6 to 7 weeks they will start their puppy vaccinations and, by 8 weeks, they should be completely weaned. You can handle the puppies from a very young age, and it is recommended that you do so in order to socialize them. Once the puppies are weaned, they can be separated from their mother. They may still need to be socialized a little before going to new homes.

Chapter Eight: Labradoodle Health and Care Guide

Feeding your Labradoodle a quality diet will help keep him in good health, but you also need to keep an eye out for medical problems so you can seek treatment as soon as a problem arises.

When your Labradoodle gets sick you obviously can't take him to your regular doctor – he needs to see a qualified and experienced veterinarian. Even when your dog isn't sick, however, he should still go to the vet every six months or so for a regular checkup. I always say that feeding your dog a high-quality diet is the best thing you can do to preserve his health, but that doesn't mean it is the only thing you should do. You also need to have a basic understanding of common health problems affecting the Labradoodle breed, so you know what signs and symptoms to look for. If your dog gets sick, you will need to take him to the vet for treatment. In this chapter, I'm going to provide you with an overview of some of the most common health problems affecting the Labradoodle breed, so you know what to look for; I'll also provide you with some important vaccination information for preventive health care.

1.) Common Health Problems for Labradoodles

The Labradoodle is a designer dog breed, as you already know, so it should make sense to you that the health problems most common in this breed will be a combination of the health problems that are common in the Poodle and in the Labrador Retriever. In this section, you will receive an overview of common conditions affecting the breed including their causes, symptoms, and treatment options. At the first sign of disease you should take your Labradoodle to the vet – the sooner you get a diagnosis and start treatment, the better your dog's chances of making a full recovery.

Some of the conditions most commonly affecting the Labradoodle breed include the following:

- Addison's Disease
- Cushing's Syndrome
- Diabetes Mellitus
- Ear Infections
- Elbow Dysplasia
- Food Allergies
- Hip Dysplasia
- Hypothyroidism
- Progressive Retinal Atrophy

- Skin Problems

In the following pages, you will receive an overview of each of these conditions including their clinical signs and symptoms, methods of diagnosis, treatment options, and prognosis information.

Addison's Disease

Also known as hypoadrenocorticism, Addison's disease is a condition caused by reduced corticosteroid secretion by the adrenal gland – a small gland in the kidney that helps to regulate certain essential bodily functions. This disease is somewhat rare in dogs but among the breeds, it is most likely to affect is the Standard Poodle – this means that the Labradoodle is at risk as well. Addison's disease typically affects young to middle-aged dogs, and it generally affects female dogs more than male dogs.

The symptoms of Addison's disease vary depending how long the disease has been going on. Some of the most common symptoms of Addison's disease in dogs include lack of appetite, lethargy, vomiting, diarrhea, weight loss, increased thirst and urination, depression, weak pulse, collapse, and hair loss. In order to diagnose Addison's disease in dogs, your vet will perform a thorough physical exam as well as various laboratory tests including a urinalysis and blood cell count.

The symptoms of Addison's disease can come on suddenly and severely – an acute episode is considered a medical emergency and requires immediate hospitalization. Treatment for Addison's disease varies from one case to another and may involve IV fluids as well as hormone replacement therapy – these therapies may need to be continued for the rest of the dog's life. After your Labradoodle recovers from an acute episode, the disease can generally be managed with hormone replacement therapy and other medical treatments to manage symptoms.

Cushing's Syndrome

Also known as hyperadrenocorticism, Cushing's disease is similar to Addison's disease in that it involves hormone production from the adrenal gland. This disease occurs when the dog's body produces too much cortisol, also known as the stress hormone. What makes Cushing's syndrome so difficult to diagnose is the fact that the symptoms overlap with various other diseases. Some of the most common symptoms seen in this disease include increased thirst and urination, increased appetite, hair loss, thinning skin, lethargy and fatigue, and panting.

Cushing's syndrome is a little more common in dogs than Addison's disease, and there are two major types: pituitary-dependent and adrenal-dependent. The first is the most common cause of Cushing's syndrome in dogs, and it involves a tumor on the pituitary gland. The adrenal-dependent type involves a tumor of the adrenal gland. Unfortunately, there is no 100% accurate method for diagnosing Cushing's syndrome in dogs. The veterinarian may perform certain tests to rule out other conditions as well as various screening tests.

Because Cushing's syndrome is generally caused by a tumor on the pituitary or adrenal gland, surgical removal is one of the most common treatments. If the tumor has spread to other parts of the body, however, surgery may not be a viable option. In most cases, dogs with Cushing's syndrome can live a normal life with medical treatment. The most common drug used to treat Cushing's syndrome in dogs is trilostane. Unfortunately, this drug is known to cause side effects so be sure to discuss all of the options with your vet before you choose a treatment.

Diabetes Mellitus

Not only can diabetes affect humans, but it can also affect dogs like the Labradoodle. Diabetes is a chronic condition in dogs, and though it can't be cured, it can be managed. Diabetes is a disease that affects the glucose-insulin connection in your dog's body. When your dog eats food, his body breaks the food down into glucose, a type of sugar. When the sugar hits his bloodstream, it stimulates the production of insulin, a hormone produced by the pancreas. Insulin helps the body utilize glucose as fuel.

In dogs with diabetes, the glucose-insulin connection doesn't work as well as it should. In some cases, the dog's body doesn't produce enough insulin and, in others, the dog's body produces enough insulin, but it isn't able to utilize it as efficiently as it should. In either case, the dog's blood sugar levels can spike dangerously high. Some of the most common symptoms of diabetes in dogs include excessive thirst, increased urination, weight loss, increased appetite, lack of energy, depression, and vomiting.

Not only can diabetes lead to the symptoms listed above, but it can also increase the dog's risk for other serious health problems. If you do not seek treatment for your dog's diabetes, he could develop cataracts, kidney failure, seizures, or ketoacidosis. Simple blood tests are generally enough to diagnose diabetes in dogs and the sooner the condition is diagnosed, the better the dog's chance of living a normal life. Dogs with diabetes may require insulin injections for the rest of their lives, though in some cases the condition can be reversed with dietary management and a healthy lifestyle.

Ear Infections

Also known as otitis externa, ear infections in dogs like the Labradoodle are relatively common. The Labradoodle has flop ears which means that they hang down on either side of the dog's head. Because the ears hang down, the inner portion of the ear gets limited airflow – if the ear gets wet, it may not dry out properly on its own, and the excess moisture can support the growth of infection-causing bacteria. If you do not address the problem promptly, it can lead to inflammation, pain, and potentially damage of the internal structures of the ear.

Some of the most common signs of ear infections in dogs include odor, discharge in the ear, shaking or rubbing the head, redness in the ear canal, tilting the head to one side, and changes in behavior such as irritability or depression. The causes of ear infections in Labradoodles can vary widely. In some cases, ear infections are the result of food allergies or other allergies. Ear infections can also be caused by a parasite (like ear mites), bacterial or yeast infections, trauma to the ear, hormonal abnormalities, and excessive moisture.

Treatment for ear infections in dogs varies depending on the cause of the problem. Antibiotics are the most common treatment for bacterial ear infections and antifungals are used for yeast infections. For ear mites, cleaning the ear is usually the first course of action. Simply squeeze a few drops of dog ear cleaning solution into the dog's ear canal then massage the base of the ear to distribute the solution. Then, use a clean cotton ball to clean and dry the ear.

Elbow Dysplasia

Elbow dysplasia in dogs is characterized by four developmental abnormalities which lead to both the malformation and the degeneration of the dog's elbow joint. This condition is very common in large-breed dogs which means that it can affect the Labradoodle. Elbow dysplasia usually manifests between 4 and 10 months of age and it is more likely to affect male dogs than females. Unfortunately, not all dogs that have these developmental abnormalities show signs of the disease – an acute (sudden) episode of elbow lameness can occur in some cases as well.

Some of the most common symptoms of elbow dysplasia in dogs include persistent or intermittent forelimb lameness (usually aggravated by exercise), stiffness or pain when extending the elbow, the tendency to hold the limb away from the body, fluid build-up in the elbow joint, and diminished range of motion. In many cases, elbow dysplasia is a genetic condition, though it may also have nutritional implications. Surgery is usually the treatment of choice and physical therapy exercises can help the dog regain mobility and flexibility of the joint.

Food Allergies

Dogs can be affected by food allergies just as much as humans can. Unfortunately, the symptoms of food allergies in dogs like the Labradoodle are easy to confuse with the symptoms of other diseases. In many cases, food allergies cause symptoms of recurrent ear infections or skin problems, not digestive issues. Approximately 10% of allergy cases in dogs are related to food and some of the most common food allergens for dogs include beef, eggs, chicken, lamb, pork, dairy, wheat, corn, soy, and fish. Many dogs with allergies are allergic to more than one food.

When it comes to treating food allergies in dogs, the best thing to do is switch your dog to a Limited Ingredient Diet (LID). This is a type of dog food made with a novel source of protein and carbohydrate (something the dog hasn't eaten before), so it is unlikely to cause a reaction. You feed the dog this diet for 12 weeks until the effects of the allergy have healed. Then you have the option of introducing potential allergens one at a time until you identify the culprit. After that, you just feed your dog a diet free from his food allergens – you can also just keep feeding him the LID.

Hip Dysplasia

This condition affects the hip joint, and it is generally caused by an abnormality in the structure of the hip joint and/or laxity of the connecting muscles, tissues, and ligaments. Over time, the hip joint becomes laxer, and the head of the femur (leg bone) can actually luxate, or slip out of its place in the hip joint. The more often this happens, the more likely the dog is to develop osteoarthritis in the joint – this can lead to pain and discomfort, even damage to the bone and joint.

Hip dysplasia is most commonly seen in large-breed dogs, but it can also occur in medium-sized breeds. It is also a disease that is more common in purebred dogs, but your Labradoodle could be at risk if both his Poodle and Labrador Retriever parents are carriers for the disease. Obesity and unbalanced nutrition can also increase your dog's risk of developing the condition. Some of the common symptoms of hip dysplasia in dogs include altered gate, stiffness or a pain in the rear joints (especially in the morning or after exercise), difficulty with stairs, and decreased activity in general. Surgery is generally the most effective long-term solution for this disease.

Hypothyroidism

Hypothyroidism is a relatively common condition in dogs, and it is caused by reduced hormone production in the dog's thyroid gland – a small gland located in the neck. Thyroid hormone plays a role in regulating many essential bodily activities, so inadequate production of this hormone can be severe. Some of the most common symptoms of hypothyroidism in dogs include weight gain, hair loss, and skin problems, especially if these symptoms seem to occur suddenly or without cause. Other potential symptoms of this condition include lethargy, mental dullness, dry coat, cold intolerance, slow heart rate, and anemia.

This condition results from impaired production and secretion of thyroid hormone from the thyroid gland. In nearly 100% of cases, the problem is due to damage to the thyroid gland, often caused by an autoimmune reaction. In some cases, however, the problem is resultant of cancerous damage to the thyroid gland or by the use of certain medications. This condition is most common in dogs between the ages of 4 and 10 and it tends to affect medium- to large-breed dogs more than smaller dogs. The best treatment for this condition is synthetic thyroid hormone replacement therapy.

Progressive Retinal Atrophy

Sometimes simply called PRA, progressive retinal atrophy is a degenerative condition affecting the retina of the dog's eye. This is a non-painful condition that usually occurs in both eyes at the same time – it also usually results in total blindness. This condition is seen in all kinds of breeds, including mixed breeds, and it is generally an inherited condition. For many dogs, the first sign of PRA is night blindness which progresses to reduced vision in all kinds of light which eventually progresses to complete and total blindness.

Unfortunately, there is no cure for progressive retinal atrophy. In many cases, however, dogs adapt well to the loss of their vision as long as their home environment remains largely unchanged. Although there is no way to prevent a dog from developing progressive retinal atrophy if he carries the gene, you can reduce the risk for future generations developing the disease by not breeding dogs that are carriers for PRA. This is one of the many reasons why DNA screening is so important for dog breeding.

Skin Problems

Skin problems are very common in Poodles which means that your Labradoodle may be at risk for these challenges as well. Cushing's syndrome has already been mentioned, and it can lead to skin problems like skin sensitivity, chronic irritation, and even hair loss. Hypothyroidism is another issue that can lead to skin problems in dogs like the Labradoodle – it may cause itchiness, and it can make the dog's coat rougher than usual. Another skin problem seen in Poodles is called sebaceous adenitis – it is most common in Toy Poodles.

Sebaceous adenitis is caused by inflammation in the oil-producing glands in your dog's skin. This condition can result in dryness, flakiness, itching, and hair loss. In some cases, it even leads to open sores and a foul odor coming from the dog's skin. This condition can be treated with topical ointments and special shampoos, but there is no permanent cure, unfortunately. Dogs like the Labradoodle can also be allergic to certain things like pollen, dust, dander, and grass which can lead to skin problems.

2.) Labradoodle Vaccination Schedule

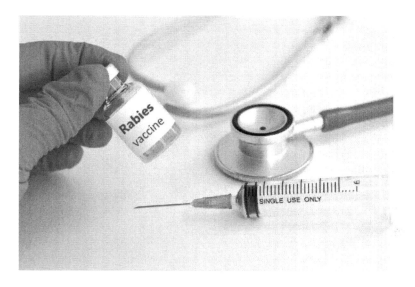

Nobody likes shots, but vaccinations are incredibly important for protecting your Labradoodle against certain deadly diseases. Don't skip the shots!

Taking the time to familiarize yourself with some of the most common conditions known to affect the Labradoodle breed will go a long way in helping to keep your dog healthy and happy. In addition to knowing what to look for and making sure that your dog sees the vet often enough, you should also ensure that he gets the vaccinations he needs. Vaccines help to protect dogs against certain contagious and deadly diseases like parvovirus, rabies (US only), and distemper. Your vet will be able to tell you exactly which vaccines your Labradoodle dog needs and when he needs them. He will need certain vaccines more frequently as a puppy, but once he grows up, he will only need booster shots once a year – some shots even come in 3- or 5-year versions.

To help you understand which vaccines your Labradoodle is likely to need and when, consult this vaccination schedule for dogs:

Vaccination Schedule for Dogs**			
Vaccine	**Doses**	**Age**	**Booster**
Rabies (US only)	1	12 weeks	annual
Distemper	3	6-16 weeks	3 years
Parvovirus	3	6-16 weeks	3 years
Adenovirus	3	6-16 weeks	3 years
Parainfluenza	3	6 weeks, 12-14 weeks	3 years
Bordetella	1	6 weeks	annual
Lyme Disease	2	9, 13-14 weeks	annual
Leptospirosis	2	12 and 16 weeks	annual
Canine Influenza	2	6-8, 8-12 weeks	annual

Chapter Nine: Showing Labradoodle Dogs

There is no denying that the Labradoodle is a gorgeous breed but because it is a designer dog it cannot be shown in AKC shows. However, you might be able to show him at a mixed breed show.

If you want to show your Labradoodle at an American Kennel Club or Kennel Club show, I have bad news – these organizations generally do not allow mixed breed dogs at their major shows. Before you despair, however, I'll tell you the good news – you might still have some options for showing your Labradoodle! Shows for mixed breed dogs are very different from those for pure breeds because many mixed breeds do not have an official breed standard. Still, designer dogs like the Labradoodle can be judged according to general standards which may vary from one competition to another. In this chapter, you'll receive some general information about show options for mixed breed dogs and some tips for preparing your Labradoodle dog for a dog show.

1.) *Showing Mixed Breed Dogs*

As I have already mentioned, you probably won't be able to show your Labradoodle at an official AKC show like the Westminster Dog Show or Crufts, the show hosted by The Kennel Club in the U.K. There are, however, other options for you to consider. <u>Below you will find an overview of some of the other dog registration organizations which host their own shows</u>:

- **The American Kennel Club** – The AKC offers some options for mixed breed dogs like the Labradoodle through their AKC Canine Partners organization. Dogs can compete in AKC events to earn titles for various dog sports including coursing, tracking, obedience, rally, and agility.

- **The Kennel Club** – In the U.K., the Kennel Club offers the Scruffts dog show for mixed breeds. In this competition, dogs have the opportunity to compete for titles like "Most Handsome Dog," "Prettiest Bitch," "Child's Best Friend," and "Golden Oldie."

- **The Mixed Breed Dog Clubs of America** – This is a national registry that accepts mixed breeds, and it offers many of the same benefits and opportunities to those dogs that the AKC offers to purebreds. The MBDCA provides a number of competitions throughout the year including rally, obedience, conformation, retriever instinct, lure coursing, and versatility.

In addition to these mixed breed dog shows, there are other canine events that designer dogs like the Labradoodle may be eligible to participate in. For example, dogs of any breed are allowed to register for competitions sponsored by the Canine Freestyle Federation or for disc dog competitions held by the International Disc Dog Handlers Association. Other organizations that hold mixed breed-friendly events include the North American Dog Agility Council, the North American Flyball Association, the United Kennel Club, and the United States Dog Agility Association.

You can find a list of crossbreed-friendly events and organizations by using the following link:

http://www.dogchannel.com/dog-activities/dog-competition/article_8002.aspx

2.) *Tips for Showing Your Labradoodle*

Showing your Labradoodle can be an exciting challenge, and it is also an excellent opportunity to spend time developing your relationship with your dog!

Although I haven't shown my own Labradoodles, I can understand the amount of thought and planning that goes into showing a dog. Your dog needs to be properly socialized, and he should have at least basic obedience training. Not only do you need to make sure that your dog is generally prepared for show, but you also have to know the specific rules and regulations for the show you're entering. <u>Here are some of the general training and socialization requirements your Labradoodle should meet before you even think about entering him in a dog show</u>:

- Your Labradoodle should be at least 12 months old – some shows have a puppy class, but not always.

- Make sure that your Labradoodle is completely housetrained and able to hold his bladder and bowels for at least 6 hours.

- The dog should be properly socialized and able to handle being in a loud, crowded setting for extended periods of time.

- Your Labradoodle needs to have basic obedience training – he needs to respond to your commands and be able to behave in public.

- The dog needs to be up to date on all of his vaccinations – if your dog isn't vaccinated, there is a very real risk that he could contract a disease from another dog at the show.

- Make sure that your Labradoodle's coat has been cleaned properly before the show and that it is entirely dry and brushed out, free from tangles.

In addition to making sure that your dog meets the requirements for the show, you should also be prepared for everything that will be happening that day. <u>Here is a list of things you may want to pack when preparing for a dog show</u>:

- Registration information
- Your dog's identification including license number and rabies vaccination info (US only)
- A dog crate and/or exercise pen
- A grooming table and any necessary supplies
- Food, water, and treats for the entire day (for both you and your dog)
- Bowls for your dog's food and water
- Toys to keep your dog occupied
- Any medications your dog may need
- Paper towels, plastic gloves, and trash bags
- A change of clothes, just in case

When you get to the dog show, keep in mind that you might spend a lot of time waiting. Take the opportunity to network with fellow dog lovers. Don't be afraid to talk to the competition! You can learn a lot from other Labradoodle owners at the show, so don't hesitate to ask questions or to observe how experienced dog showers do things.

Chapter Ten: Labradoodle Dog Care Sheet

As dignified as the Labradoodle looks this breed also has a bit of a clownish side. You never know what he might do next!

By now you have learned just about everything I can teach you about the Labradoodle breed, and I hope that you see just how amazing these dogs can be! When you bring your own Labradoodle puppy home for the first time, you should expect to have an adjustment period where the two of you start getting to know each other. As you and your puppy move forward through life, you may find that you need to reference key Labradoodle facts and information from this book. Instead of flipping through the whole thing I've compiled a Labradoodle dog care sheet in this chapter with all of the bits and pieces you'll need most.

1.) Labradoodle Information Overview

Pedigree: cross between the Labrador Retriever and the Poodle (any of the three sizes)

AKC Group: not AKC-recognized

Breed Size: miniature, medium, and standard

Height: 14 to 16 inches (35.5 to 40.6 cm) Miniature; 17 to 20 inches (43.2 to 50.8 cm) Medium; 21 to 24 inches (53.5 to 61 cm) Standard

Weight: 15 to 25 pounds (6.8 to 11.3 kg) Miniature; 30 to 45 pounds (13.6 to 20.4 kg) Medium; 50 to 65 pounds (22.7 to 29.5 kg) Standard

Coat Length: short, medium, or long

Coat Texture: fine, wool, or fleece

Color: any color including white, peach, cream, apricot, gold, tan, brown, beige, red, black, silver; solid, parti-color, or bi-color

Eyes and Nose: dark brown or black

Ears: flopped ears, well covered in fur

Tail: generally carried high

Temperament: friendly, lively, people-oriented, active

Strangers: may be shy around strangers but warms up quickly once introduced

Other Dogs: generally good with other dogs

Other Pets: generally gets along with other pets

Training: intelligent and very trainable; Miniature size may take longer to housetrain than other dogs

Exercise Needs: fairly active or energetic; needs plenty of daily exercise and mental stimulation

Health Conditions: Addison's disease, Cushing's syndrome, hypothyroidism, progressive retinal atrophy, skin problems, food allergies, hip dysplasia, elbow dysplasia, ear infections, diabetes, etc.

Lifespan: average 10 to 15 years

2.) Labradoodle Home Requirements Overview

Space Requirements: can be adaptable to a variety of living situations with adequate exercise

Energy Level: moderate to high energy

Attention Needs: very people-oriented, should not be left alone for long periods of time

Exercise Requirements: a 30-minute daily walk is absolutely required, additional playtime and exercise recommended

Crate: highly recommended; line with a comfy blanket or plush dog bed

Crate Size: just large enough to stand up, sit down, turn around, and lie down in comfortably

Toys: provide an assortment; be sure to include chew toys as well as interactive toys

Confinement: use a puppy playpen or a small spare room to provide your puppy with some personal space

Food/Water Bowls: place them in your puppy's area; stainless steel is the best material

Shedding Level: low to moderate

Brushing: at least several times a week; use a wire-pin brush and work through tangles with a comb

Trimming): puppy clip or pet clip recommended for easy maintenance; show dogs may be kept longer

Grooming Frequency: recommended every 6 to 8 weeks

Bathing: no more than every two weeks; bathing too frequently can dry out the dog's skin

Cleaning Ears: as needed, check at least once a week; use dog-friendly ear cleaning solution and cotton balls

Trimming Nails: once a week; trim the minimal amount needed to prevent overgrowth

3.) Labradoodle Nutritional Information

Diet Type: carnivorous; derives most of its nutrition from animal sources

Primary Nutrients: protein, fat, carbohydrates, water, vitamins, and minerals

Protein: made up of amino acids, supports growth and development of muscle and tissue

Amino Acids: total of 22, 10 of which are essential (need to come from the diet)

Fat: most concentrated source of energy; best from animal sources like chicken fat and fish oil

Carbohydrate: amount should be limited; best from digestible sources like whole grains (brown rice and oatmeal) or gluten-free sources (potatoes, peas, sweet potatoes)

Minimum Requirements (Puppy): 22% protein, 8% fat

Minimum Requirements (Adult): 18% protein, 5% fat

Ideal Range (Puppy): 22% to 32% protein, 10% to 25% fat

Ideal Range (Adult): 30% protein, up to 20% fat

Dog Food Points of Comparison: AAFCO statement of nutritional adequacy, guaranteed analysis, ingredients list

Recommended Proteins: fresh meats, poultry, eggs, seafood, meat meals

Recommended Fat: animal fat and fish oils

Nutrients: best from natural sources rather than synthetic supplements

Beneficial Additives: dried fermentation products, chelated minerals, vitamin supplements

Ingredients to Avoid: corn, wheat, and soy; artificial colors, flavors, and preservatives

Calorie Needs: varies by size, age, and activity level

Meals per Day: two or three

Feeding Tips: choose a formula designed for dogs of its size; feed several small meals rather than one large meal

4.) *Labradoodle Breeding Information*

Age of First Heat: around 6 months (or earlier)

Breeding Age (male): no younger than 1 year, no older than 12 years

Breeding Age (female): no younger than 18 months, no older than 8 years

Heat (Estrus) Cycle: 14 to 21 days

Frequency: twice a year, every 6 to 7 months; some small breeds have 3 cycles per year

Greatest Fertility: 7 to 10 days into the cycle

Gestation Period: average 63 days

Pregnancy Detection: possible after 21 days, best to wait 28 days before exam

Feeding Pregnant Dogs: maintain normal diet until week 5 or 6 then slightly increase rations

Signs of Labor: body temperature drops below normal 100° to 102°F (37.7° to 38.8°C), may be as low as 98°F (36.6°C); dog begins nesting in a dark, quiet place

Contractions: period of 10 minutes in waves of 3 to 5 followed by a period of rest

Whelping: puppies are born in 1/2 hour increments following 10 to 30 minutes of forceful straining

Puppies: born with eyes and ears closed; completely dependent on mother; sleep and nurse all day

Puppy Development: crawling day 7 to 14; walking by day 21; sampling solid food at week 3, weaned by week 8

Litter Size: 4 to 15 puppies, 8 average

Weaning: start offering puppy food soaked in water at 5 to 6 weeks; fully weaned by 8 weeks

Socialization: start as early as possible to prevent puppies from being nervous as an adult

Conclusion

Nothing is cuter than a Labradoodle puppy, but you must remember that caring for a dog is a big responsibility. Do your research before you bring home a pet!

Well, if I haven't convinced you by now that the Labradoodle is one of the best dog breeds there are, I don't think I'm going to. I have done my best to do more than just tell you why these dogs are so great – I have tried to show you what it is like to own a Labradoodle in hopes that you will come to feel as strongly for this breed as I have. It wasn't all that long ago that I was like you – unfamiliar with the Labradoodle and a little bit skeptical about mixed breed dogs. But I came to my senses and now I know the truth – that Labradoodles are a wonderful breed that anyone would be lucky to own!

So, if you think that the Labradoodle just might be the perfect pet for you, I want to encourage you to follow that line of thinking! Do not rush out and buy the first puppy you come across, however – take the time to do some of your own research about the breed. I have done my best to provide you with all of the information you need to get a feel for the breed, but dog ownership is a big responsibility and not one that should be entered into lightly! Unless you are able to devote yourself to caring for a Labradoodle for the duration of his entire life, I don't think it is the right pet for you.

My goal in writing this book was to help others come to see the beauty that is the Labradoodle. Not only are these dogs physically beautiful (just look at that curly coat!) but they are also beautiful on the inside. I am convinced that my Sandy and Layla are the perfect specimens of dog-hood, and I know that the first time you set eyes on your Labradoodle puppy that you will feel the same way about yours. I have done all that I can to teach you about this breed, so it is up to you now to take this information and run with it! I wish you and your future Labradoodle the best of luck and a lifetime of happiness!

Index

A

AAFCO 89, 163

accessories 46, 48

active 15, 17, 18, 20, 25, 27, 28, 55, 65, 75, 78, 83, 158, 159

activity 66, 163

Addison's disease 19, 21, 26, 28, 131, 133, 159

Adenovirus 146

adoption 47, 70, 71, 72, 73

afterbirth 125

age 7

agility 13, 150

AKC 4, 5

AKC Canine Partners 150

allergy 18, 23, 55, 140

American Kennel Club 4

American Labradoodle 30, 31, 58

amino acids 86, 162

Animal Movement License 41

antibodies 48, 125

appearance 5, 6, 23

artificial additives 91

assistance dog 29

attention 13, 18, 26, 44, 55, 74, 91, 109

Australian Labradoodle 31, 62, 63, 72

autoimmune 142

award 4

B

B.F. Skinner 106

backcrossed 119

backcrossing 119

bacteria 47, 99

bathe 23, 98

behavior 5, 17, 105, 106, 109, 110, 120, 137

benefits 151

Best in Show 4

birth 118, 121, 122, 124, 125

bitch 5, 7

black 12, 15, 20, 23, 27, 35, 158

blindness 143

blood 101

body 6, 7

bodyweight 92, 163

booster shots 146

Bordatella 146

bowls 46, 47, 48, 52

breed 5, 6, 7, 49, 51, 59, 60, 61, 118, 119, 120, 129, 145, 150, 151

breed standard 31, 63, 149

breeder 29, 47, 49, 56, 59, 60, 61, 63, 65, 66, 67, 68, 83

breeding 6, 8, 26, 29, 35, 45, 55, 58, 59, 60, 61, 96, 99, 116, 118, 119, 122, 143

brown 6, 12, 15, 20, 23, 27, 34, 36, 87, 158, 162

brush 6, 18, 23, 49, 52, 80, 96, 97, 98, 100, 161

C

cage 5

cancer 19

Canine Freestyle Federation 151

Canine Influenza 146

carbohydrate 85, 87, 91, 140

care 4, 51, 58, 121

care sheet 157

castrate 7

cataracts 14, 15, 135

Cesar Milan 104

checkup 127

chew 48, 160

chewing 13

children .... 12, 17, 18, 25, 54 chocolate Labradoodle 34

coat 6, 1, 5, 6, 7, 8, 12, 15, 16, 17, 20, 23, 24, 27, 29, 34, 37, 49, 52, 55, 63, 80, 84, 86,
96, 97, 98, 102, 142, 144, 154, 158, 167

collar 48, 52

color 1, 6, 7, 15, 20, 24, 27, 34, 35, 36, 37, 70, 120, 158

coloration 7

coloring 5

colors 7, 91, 163

colostrum 125

comb 6, 18, 49, 80, 97, 161

command 6, 113

commands 13, 15, 107, 108, 111, 153

competition 151

complications 122

conception 120

condition 6, 66, 93, 96, 131, 135, 136, 139, 141, 142, 143, 144

conditions 130

conformation 151

congenital 14, 26, 58

corn 84, 88, 91, 140, 163

corticosteroid 131

costs 39, 45, 46, 47, 48, 50, 51, 52, 53, 88

crate 46, 47, 76, 77, 79, 80, 112, 113, 114, 154

crossbreed 151

Crufts 150

Cushing's syndrome 19, 21, 26, 28, 133, 144, 159

cycle 120, 124, 164

D

dam 5, 7

degeneration 139

dental 19, 21, 99

depression 131, 135, 137

designer dog 2, 22, 24, 77, 118, 129, 148

destructive 13, 26, 78

Diabetes 129, 135

diagnosis 130

diarrhea 60, 66
diet..87, 88, 162, 164
dietary fiber 87
digestive problems.. 83
discharge.. 120
disease 19, 48, 58, 100, 122, 129, 131, 133, 135, 139, 141, 143, 153
disorder 6
distemper.. 146
Distemper 146
dog bed..46, 47, 77, 80, 160
dog breed... 1
dog food..51, 82, 88, 89, 90, 140
dog shows 151
dog sports 12, 13, 16, 17, 18, 54, 79, 150
Dog Whisperer.. 104
dogs 5, 6
dominance training.. 104, 106
double coat 5, 15

E

ear6, 7
ear infections 26, 28, 99, 137, 140, 159
ear mites.. 137, 138
ears 6, 15, 20, 24, 27, 66, 99, 126, 137, 158, 165
eating.. 8
eggs...86, 120, 121, 140, 163
elbow 15, 26, 28, 139, 159
energy.. 13, 25, 34, 77, 78, 86, 93, 125, 135, 160, 162
epilepsy...14, 15, 19, 26
escape.. 13
estrus cycle 119
exercise...... 13, 14, 15, 17, 20, 25, 28, 44, 55, 56, 75, 77, 78, 79, 139, 141, 154, 159, 160
eye 4
eye conditions.. 14, 26
eyes.. 4, 66, 165

F

F1 118, 119

face 4, 24, 59

family 6, 12, 16, 19, 25, 29, 54, 105

fat 87, 90, 162, 163

fats 85, 86, 90, 92

feet 24

female 4, 5, 7, 8, 32, 68, 119, 120, 121, 122, 131, 164

fluid 139

flyball 13

food 8, 19, 21, 26, 28, 45, 46, 47, 48, 51, 52, 55, 76, 77, 80, 82, 83, 84, 85, 86, 87, 88, 89, 90, 91, 93, 94, 110, 114, 123, 126, 135, 137, 140, 154, 159, 165

food allergies 19, 21, 26, 28, 137, 140, 159

foot 7

formula 92, 163

fur 15, 20, 27, 49, 66, 158

G

gastric torsion 14, 15, 26

gene 5

genealogy 7

generation 31, 118, 119

genetic 6, 58, 122

genetics 11, 22, 31, 36

gentle 1, 9, 15, 18, 24, 25, 29, 54, 100, 108

gestation period 121, 124

gland 131, 133, 142

golden Labradoodle 35

grooming 18, 46, 49, 51, 52, 55, 74, 96, 100, 154

growth 7, 162

guide dog 29

H

hair .... 4, 5, 6, 7, 8 hair loss...131, 133, 142, 144

harness 48

health................ 5, 19, 26, 45, 55, 60, 66, 82, 84, 85, 86, 87, 89, 122, 127, 128, 129, 135

health problems..55, 89, 128, 129, 135

healthy..49, 66, 87, 122, 145

heart disease 14, 15

heat... 119, 120

hereditary 122

hip6, 14, 15, 26, 28, 141, 159

hip dysplasia 14, 26, 28, 141, 159

Hip Dysplasia... 6

history.. 10, 71

hormone 132, 133, 135, 142

house 4, 5

housebreaking 69, 103, 112

housetrain...19, 20, 28, 159

housing 75

humane society 72

hybrid.. 118, 119

hypothyroidism...19, 21, 26, 28, 142, 159

Hypothyroidism 15, 21, 28, 159

I

illness 66

immune.. 48, 86, 125

infection.. 99, 137

information 40, 48, 50, 53, 59, 60, 66, 130, 154

ingredients..84, 88, 89, 90, 91, 94, 163

initial costs 46

injury.. 66

insulin 135, 136

intelligence 1, 16, 29, 102

intelligent...15, 20, 28, 159

International Disc Dog Handlers Association 151

J

joint.. 6, 139, 141

K

kennel 5
Kennel Club...11, 148, 150, 151
kibble 92
kidney 131, 135

L

Lab 13, 25, 26, 31, 46, 68
label 90
labor.. 125
Labrador Retriever.... 6, 2, 9, 11, 12, 13, 26, 29, 30, 31, 32, 33, 34, 35, 36, 60, 62, 78, 97, 129, 141, 158
large-breed 14, 92, 93, 120, 139, 141, 142
leash.. 48
legs... 6
length 120, 121
Leptospirosis 146
lethargic 65
licensing 40, 41
lifespan 19, 26
Limited Ingredient Diet 140
litter 8, 58, 116, 118, 119, 121, 122, 123, 126
loyal 16, 25

M

maintenance 13, 18, 25, 74, 75, 98, 161
male 7, 8, 32, 68, 120, 121, 122, 131, 139, 164
malformation 139
markings 7

mating.. 121

mats 18, 97

meals 90, 93, 113, 163

medications 142, 154

Medium Labradoodle 32, 92

mental stimulation 13, 15, 17, 20, 25, 28, 79, 159

microchipping 46

milk 8

minerals 85, 87, 91, 162, 163

Mini Labradoodle.. 32

Miniature Australian Labradoodle 32

Miniature Labradoodle 32, 33, 67, 68, 92

Miniature Poodle 16, 67

mixed breed.. 11, 148, 151, 167

mobility.. 139

monthly costs 46

N

nail clippers.. 49

nails.. 100, 101

neuter 46, 49

night blindness.. 143

North American Dog Agility Council 151

nose 109, 110

nutrients 88, 125

nutrition 87, 162

nutritional deficiencies 89

nutritional needs 84, 85, 88, 89

O

obedience 13, 70, 150, 151, 152, 153

obesity 14, 15

odor 66, 137, 144

osteochondrosis 14, 15

outer coat 8

ovaries 8

P

pain 137, 139, 141

Parainfluenza 146

parasite 137

parent 2, 5, 8, 9, 11, 22, 38, 58, 119

parti-colored 24

parvovirus 145

Parvovirus 146

patellar luxation 14, 15

pedigree..32, 60, 62, 63

personality 6, 1, 9, 11, 16, 18, 25, 26, 34, 64, 71

pet.....6, 2, 19, 29, 40, 44, 46, 51, 54, 58, 59, 83, 84, 88, 89, 90, 91, 93, 98, 161, 166, 167

pet clip 161

Pet Poison Control 94

pets..15, 20, 27, 159

playpen 160

playtime 25, 78, 160

Poodle 6, 2, 9, 11, 16, 17, 18, 19, 20, 22, 23, 24, 25, 26, 29, 30, 31, 32, 33, 35, 36, 37, 38,
    46, 52, 54, 60, 62, 67, 68, 78, 96, 97, 119, 129, 131, 141, 158

positive reinforcement 104, 109, 110, 112

praise 110, 111, 114

pregnancy 118, 121, 123, 124

pregnant 120, 121

preservatives 91, 163

price.. 46, 47, 84

probiotics.. 91

prognosis 130

progressive retinal atrophy..14, 15, 19, 21, 28, 143, 159

pros and cons...39, 54, 70, 71

protein 85, 86, 87, 90, 91, 140, 162

punish 105, 108

punishment...105, 106, 107, 108, 112

puppies .... 6, 8, 48, 60, 65, 66, 118, 121, 124, 125, 126, 165 puppy.....6, 2, 18, 24, 25, 38, 45, 46, 47, 48, 51, 54, 56, 58, 59, 60, 61, 63, 65, 66, 67, 69, 70, 75, 76, 77, 79, 80, 83, 98, 112, 113, 114, 125, 126, 146, 153, 156, 160, 161, 165, 166, 167

puppy mill 58

purchase price 45

purebred 4, 118, 119

Q

qualities 1, 2, 14, 38, 46

quarantine 41

R

rabies 40, 41, 146, 154

reaction.. 140, 142

record 7

red Labradoodle... 36

registration 11, 59, 150

registry... 4

reinforce 106

requirements 25, 40, 41, 74, 75, 79, 87, 89, 90, 92, 153, 154

rescue 13, 47, 58, 59, 71, 73

reward 106, 107, 109, 111, 114

rewards.. 110

S

schedule.. 146

scientific training 104, 107

shampoo 49, 80, 98

shed 18, 23, 97

shock collar.. 105

show 4, 61, 65, 101, 125, 153, 154

show clip... 98

signs .... 60, 66, 100, 114, 120, 124, 125, 128, 130, 137, 139 sire 5, 7

size 16, 19, 24, 26, 28, 32, 33, 67, 68, 70, 81, 83, 92, 126, 159, 163

skin 5, 7, 14, 15, 19, 21, 26, 28, 48, 86, 96, 97, 133, 140, 142, 144, 159, 161

skin allergies 14, 15

skin problems 19, 21, 28, 140, 142, 144, 159

skull 4

small-breed 92, 93

smart 13, 17, 18, 55, 102, 108, 110

social 22, 42, 44

socialization 18, 153

soy 88, 91, 140, 163

spay 7, 46, 49, 119

standard 61

Standard Australian Labradoodle 32

Standard Poodle 17, 78

stranger 23

strangers 20, 27, 65, 159

stress 104, 106, 108, 133

supplements 91, 163

surgery 8, 46, 49

swelling 66, 120

swimming 13

symptoms 128, 129, 130, 131, 133, 135, 139, 140, 141, 142

T

tail 5, 6, 15, 23, 66

tangle 49

tangles 18, 97, 154, 161

teeth 4, 99, 100, 126

temperament 1, 9, 18, 23, 24, 29, 63, 102

temperature 124, 125, 164

texture 23, 66

therapy 13, 132, 139, 142

thirst 131, 133, 135

time 6, 11, 25, 44, 46, 55, 56, 59, 61, 71, 79, 83, 84, 98, 100, 101, 106, 107, 110, 112,
113, 114, 116, 121, 124, 126, 140, 141, 143, 145, 152, 153, 154, 156, 160, 167

toy 25, 106, 111

Toy Poodle 16, 46, 67

toys 46, 48, 52, 160

training 13, 18, 25, 29, 47, 54, 70, 76, 77, 79, 93, 102, 104, 105, 106, 107, 108, 109, 110, 112, 113, 115, 152, 153

training sequence 110

treatment 127, 128, 129, 130, 134, 135, 138, 139, 142

treats 51, 93, 105, 109, 113, 154

tricks 109

trim 6

trimming 5

types 10, 30, 62, 107, 133

U

undercoat 5, 15

United States 4, 151

urination 120

urine marking... 120

V

vaccination.. 40, 146, 154

vaccinations 45, 46, 49, 69, 82, 83, 126, 145, 153

vet49, 51, 66, 88, 101, 125, 145

vet clinic.. 49

veterinarian 93, 122, 124, 127, 133

vitamins 85, 87, 91, 162

von Willebrand's disease 26

vulva 120

W

walk 114, 126

water..................................13, 14, 19, 46, 47, 48, 76, 77, 80, 85, 98, 114, 154, 162, 165

wean 126

weather .... 6, 13 weight 32, 87, 93, 124, 131, 135, 142

Westminster Dog Show 150

wheat..88, 91, 140, 163

whelp 121, 124, 125

white 4, 5, 7

white Labradoodle 36

wire-pin brush.. 49

working 16, 17, 18, 97

Y

yeast 137, 138

yellow 6, 12, 23, 35, 36, 37

Yorkshire Terrier 119

22217071R00107

Printed in Great Britain
by Amazon